Acts of Resistance

The Poetry of U.A.Fanthorpe

U.A.Fanthorpe
© Mark Gerson/National Portrait Gallery, London.

Acts of Resistance

The Poetry of U.A.Fanthorpe

Elizabeth Sandie

PETERLOO POETS

First published in 2009 by Peterloo Poets
The Old Chapel, Sand Lane, Calstock,
Cornwall PL18 9QX, U.K.

**A catalogue record for this book is available
from the British Library**

ISBN 978-1-904324-53-9

Printed in Great Britain
By 4word Ltd, Unit15, Baker's Park, Bristol BS13 7TT

ACKNOWLEDGEMENTS

I am indebted to many people: first to Peter Sansom at The Poetry Business for commissioning a chapter on Fanthorpe's work in 2000. My plans for this longer study grew out of that work. They were given voice and a receptive ear during walks in North Yorkshire with my late friend, Isabel Mclean. She was finalising research for her own scholarly book on *The Life and Works of Joseph Foord*. Isabel shared my appreciation of Fanthorpe's poetry and found time to encourage and give rigorous feedback on my early chapters until her untimely death in 2006.

Several other former colleagues from York St John University have had a significant influence: Mary Eagleton first introduced me to the problematic issues surrounding the publication and reception of women's writing; Lynne Cameron and Jo Vicary have offered helpful advice; Linda Hoy, Royal Literary Fellow, gave thoughtful encouragement and detailed feedback on drafts of this study during her writing residency at YSJ; last but not least my thanks go to Paul Mills whose affectionate support and painstaking comments have been invaluable throughout.

I am indebted to U.A. Fanthorpe, not only for the poetry, but for being so generous with her time for interviews in 2002, a visit funded by York St John's research department, and for giving me access to scripts of unpublished talks and lectures, hunted out by her partner Dr Rosie Bailey. The discovery of U.A.'s Marvell lecture was a 'eureka' moment in tying in my initial ideas of 'outsiderness' in the opening chapter with my thoughts on U.A.'s place in the canon in the final chapter. Hearing U.A. and Rosie's 'double act' in York at our *riverlines* series in 2004 was particularly significant. Thanks, too, to Rosie for her hospitality, for checking my draft for factual accuracy and for her meticulous proof reading.

My family and friends will know how much I have appreciated their love, support, and company. To those who have been eagerly awaiting this book, thanks for your patience.

Thanks finally to Peterloo Poets; I have accepted editorial advice on minor details, but not on the title – my own 'act of resistance' was to insist on this.

Elizabeth Sandie
July 2008

For Harry,

and in memoriam Jill McWilliam (1943-2008)

CONTENTS

Abstract

The opening chapter of this study explores the thematic and stylistic territory of U.A.Fanthorpe's poetry. It identifies attitudes of outsiderness, resistance and subversion which it relates to her early childhood experiences of war, the influence of her barrister father and her awareness of 'difference' in her sexual identity. It goes on to consider four other key elements of her work.

Chapter Two considers the way Fanthorpe constructs herself as a witness, a translator of other lives and worlds. Her poetry, nonetheless, acknowledges the unreliability of the witness and the struggle, shared with visual artists, to find a language adequate to translate lived experience onto page or canvas. This very process of acts of attention to others illuminates the sensibility of the observer despite the poet's desire to remain unseen.

The third chapter reveals Fanthorpe as a poet for whom England, its language, history, people and traditions matter; yet her work which so frequently investigates the past simultaneously reveals an anxiety for England now. She sees a fragile land subject to coastal and cultural erosions, threatened by global instabilities.

The fourth considers the tensions between the dark and the light in Fanthorpe's work. She can make the reader laugh out loud with her irreverent rewritings of familiar stories. Yet, like Hopkins, Fanthorpe knows 'the mind has mountains, no-man-fathomed.' Much of her writing has been 'to explore an area of darkness in the mind'. Her celebrations of life, love, language, people, in the ordinariness and extraordinariness of their experience shine out against this darkness.

The final chapter examines the paradox of an outsider poet who has managed to become an establishment figure. It asks why this poet, who is so popular with readers, audiences and other poets, is not more visible in critical overviews of the period. What is her connection with or distance from a literary tradition? How has she managed to be both marginal and mainstream?

Prefatory Note

The page references in this study refer to U.A.Fanthorpe's *Collected Poems 1978-2003* published in 2005 by Peterloo Poets. The first mention of any poem considered in detail also gives a reference to its first appearance in an individual collection. The following abbreviations are used:

Side Effects (SE)
Standing To (ST)
Voices Off (VO)
A Watching Brief (AWB)
Neck-Verse (NV)
Safe As Houses (SAH)
Consequences (C)
Christmas Poems (ChP)
Queueing for the Sun (Q)
Collected Poems 1978-2003 (CP)

I have also abbreviated references to autobiographical pieces and essays after their first mention.

An Honest Trade (AHT)
Autobiography of a Reader (AOR)
A Scrappy Little Harvest (ASLH)
Hospitalspeak (H)
Slow Learner (SL)
The Uses of Ignorance (TUOI)
War, Poetry, The Child (WPC)

Full details of these and other publications by and about U.A.Fanthorpe are given in the Select Bibliography beginning on page 163. Anyone who knows Fanthorpe's views on what can be done to poetry by academics will understand that my excitement on beginning this study was tempered by some trepidation. I hope I have avoided any alienating jargon. I have seen this study as a way of sharing some insights into the range and craftsmanship of Fanthorpe's poetry with the 'common reader' as well as with students of poetry.

Chapter One

Acts of resistance and subversion

'I felt very strongly that I wanted to be subversive: saw myself as being against power-holders, with no weapons except words and laughter.'

(U.A.F. in conversation with Marilyn Hacker, 1989:163)

Outsiderness

Much of U.A.Fanthorpe's poetic identity comes from a sense of 'outsiderness' and from her empathy with the voiceless in society. Her poetry takes marginal characters and places them centre stage: the very old, the mad, the failures, the dispossessed. She allies herself with Wordsworth who, she says:

> confronts someone marginalised by society, an idiot boy, a small poor girl, a leech gatherer and manages the story in such a way as to subvert the values of society, including presumably those of the poet. The marginal ones come out on top (Hospitalspeak:34).

Fanthorpe is well aware of poetry itself as a subversive medium:

> A poet whether he chooses or not is a smuggler. He imports things clandestinely which are not supposed to have got through the customs (An Honest Trade).

In her unpublished essay, 'The Uses Of Ignorance' she acknowledges that any individual poem can 'rebel; take the law into its own hands; behave as if it had autonomy'. She likens the process of writing a poem to:

> travelling through a tunnel and not being able to see the light at the end. If I could see the light at the end there'd be no poem; the whole process would be too straightforward. I have to believe the light is there, that the poem has a point; that it's going to come clean with me.

Fanthorpe realises that 'this is contrary to most things society stands for. It's irrational, arbitrary, confused, unscientific. It also values ignorance.' She goes on to express her resistance to the particular type of 'knowingness' the contemporary world values so highly:

> Hemmed in between the journalist, the advertiser, the politician, the academic, we're constantly being told what to do, what to buy, what to

think, by people who seem to know. Their speech is cliché. Their message propaganda (TUOI:14).

A fascination with language and contrasting registers permeates her work. She explains how she was 'tipped over into poetry' when working as a hospital receptionist:

> I could think of no other way of responding to this babel of voices, this jumble of codes, everyone wanting something and most of them held back, because of illness or etiquette, from the effective spark of communication (H:33).

In listening to the patients she recognised that 'the gaps and repetitions of their speech, their sallies into and out of sense had a kind of wild poetry' (H:32).

Side Effects

The first hospital poems formed a substantial section of her first volume *Side Effects* (1978), which brought her immediate popular and critical acclaim. She was hailed by Charles Causley as 'a new and original voice in English poetry, clear, distinctive and remarkably assured' (Wainwright, 1995:76). The title *Side Effects* simultaneously suggests pathologies and point of view. As the American poet and critic Marilyn Hacker commented, this was a setting seldom seen in poetry:

> a hospital seen from its underside: nurses, cleaners, orderlies, in-and-out-patients, the routine, the separations, the stasis, with the unifying voice that of an observer neither in danger nor in power, an underling (Hacker, 1989:148).

The debunking of pretension, hypocrisy, bureaucracy and the pleasure of subversion are prominent in Fanthorpe's poetry. She is perhaps best known for her witty dramatic monologues. Like Browning, 'she communicates to the reader far more than the idiosyncrasies of the individual through whom she speaks' (Vernon Scannell in Wainwright, 1995:81).

It was with one of these monologues that Fanthorpe first came to public attention. Her poem 'Not My Best Side' won second prize in *Phoenix* magazine's *poem about a painting* competition in 1975. *Phoenix* was founded and edited by Harry Chambers while still a student at Liverpool. He then moved to Manchester where he founded Peterloo Poets, taking its name from the massacre of protesters at St Peter's Field, Manchester, dubbed the "Battle of Peterloo", which took place in 1819 (four years after Waterloo). Uccello's 'Saint George and the Dragon' hangs in the National Gallery and is reproduced on the cover of *Side Effects*, Fanthorpe's first Peterloo volume. This small independent press, now based in Cornwall, has subsequently published seven further individual volumes of Fanthorpe's poetry, as well as a *Selected Poems* and a *Collected Poems 1978-2003*.

In 'Not My Best Side' Fanthorpe creates voices for the three main figures from the painting, the dragon, the girl and the hero. 'Not my best side' is the opening gambit of the dragon, offering a critique of his own portrait. He's far from being a satisfied customer. 'The artist didn't give me a chance to / Pose properly... / Poor chap. He had this obsession with / Triangles, so he left off two of my / Feet.' Though he 'hadn't commented at the time', in retrospect the dragon admits to being 'sorry for the bad publicity' (SE:38; CP:42).

The poem helps the reader see Uccello's painting afresh. The eye is directed, via the dragon's voice, to details that might have been overlooked, 'Why should she have me literally on a string?' and to see aspects of the structure and rhythm of the composition, the pictorial conventions of Uccello's day, its narrative style, its *ways* of telling. Through St George's voice we also hear the distance between the chivalric codes of the mediaeval world and the contemporary obsession with self-promotion and materialism. The tripartite structure of the poem echoes the painter's 'obsession with / Triangles.' Just as there is a line which takes the eye through the painting, so there are connecting threads, which link the three sections of the poem. The girl has far from maidenly thoughts:

> It's hard for a girl to be sure if
> She wants to be rescued. I mean I quite
> Took to the dragon. ... /
> > ... He was
> So nicely physical, with his claws
> And lovely green skin, and that sexy tail. (SE:38; CP:42)

Saint George, with 'diplomas in Dragon / Management and Virgin Reclamation' tells her in his egoistic way:

> I'm qualified and equipped to the
> Eyebrow. So why be difficult?
> Don't you want to be killed and / or rescued
> In the most contemporary way? Don't
> You want to carry out the roles
> That sociology and myth have designed for you?' (CP:43)

The girl doesn't get the chance to bellow NO! The hero doesn't bother to wait for an answer, sweeps her needs to one side, ends this trilogy of monologues with: ·

> What, in any case, does it matter what
> You want? You're in my way. (CP:43)

Shifting perspectives, whether of time, gender, or status, make a crucial difference to the way a subject is narrated. What the monster sees in derogatory terms as 'A horse with a deformed neck and square hoofs' is seen by its owner as 'the latest model, with / Automatic transmission and built-in obsolescence.' In re-visioning this picture and retelling its story in a contemporary idiom Fanthorpe is being very wittily and perhaps irreverently entertaining about an iconic subject at the heart of the construction of Englishness. Fanthorpe's continued interrogation of the nature of Englishness will be the focus of a later chapter of this study. The age of chivalry has clearly gone. Gone too is the age when women were seen as passive victims awaiting rescue. Despite its witty surface this poem presents an incisive image of contemporary society, its jargons, its changing sexual morality and fashions, its goal-oriented consumerism, its emphasis on self-image, its self-seeking. It is not insignificant that the voice she found for St George was modelled on a type of Thatcherian business man. Fanthorpe has a sharp satirical eye and ear to record subtle changes in social / sexual / political / literary attitudes. She is particularly scathing about the increased materialism of the Thatcherite years and their aftermath and deplores what she perceives as the reductiveness of contemporary society.

Mere mortals

'What's important to me is *people*' Fanthorpe has asserted. 'If a landscape appears in my work it's because people have made it or done something to it' (Pitt,1994:14). 'It is the human voice and human words that matter to me' (ASLH:6). Fanthorpe witnesses the griefs and triumphs of workaday lives with tremendous com-passion, fully aware that people can be at the mercy, not only of the natural elements, poverty, ill health or accidental misfortune, but also the speculators and war mongers, who rob them of real choices. Whilst the history books focus on the named victors of wars, she is concerned with the 'Hundreds And Thousands' (CP:358) of name-less dead. She is also concerned to record that, 'what matters is that people live / The ordinary all-in-a-day's-work life of peace' (CP:357). She knows that to be alive is to be, 'Marvellous rich. An offer not to be repeated' (CP:358). She senses both 'the un-repeatable marvel of each second' (CP:314) as well as 'the unpretending minutes of bleak lives' (CP:291). She acknowledges imperatives of ordinary lives that history books omit, of love, light, landscape, weather, time, cats.

Fanthorpe has a good ear for voices. She has the knack of capturing the idiom, dialect, intonation, pace and quirky idiosyncrasies of speech which make people special. She's aware of nuances of movement, gesture, body language; so the voices come with stage directions which are eloquent too. Some voices, however, are more important than others; in her poem 'Against Speech', with a reversal of the normal hierarchies, she lists as 'disposable', 'the expensive eloquence / Of 'QC's, DJ's, MP's' (C:32; CP:367). At the theatre, for example, in the poem 'Afterwards', she's much less interested in 'the principalities, the powers, the politicians, / The ones who pose in the spotlight /... the rich and the Richards, / Rehearsing ... / The precise strut that registers power' than the off-stage drama of the cleaners 'laughing and mopping up' (C:65; CP:394).

Her monologues often recast familiar biblical, Shakespearean or classical stories in a new light, giving their characters a contemporary voice. In her second volume she has a punningly titled sequence 'Only Here for the Bier' which she wrote because she was 'interested to see what the masculine world of Shakespeare's tragedies would look like from the woman's angle' (ST:49; CP:94). Also, whilst teaching in a girls' school, the paucity of roles for women in the plays became an irritant. The idea for the sequence was begun, as she explains to Angela Pitt, (1994:13) after leaving a lecture by painter Monica Sjöo which revealed the totally different perspective on the world of women painters. This left her wondering about a literary equivalent.

This sequence gives us four monologues: Gertrude's thoughts on Ophelia as her prospective daughter-in-law; Regan 'The King's Daughter' in *King Lear* reflecting, 'that being a middle sister is tiresome'; Emilia, an 'Army Wife' from *Othello* and a 'Waiting Gentlewoman' from *Macbeth* (ST:50-53; CP:95-8). Fanthorpe found very different voices for these characters by thinking about how women talk today, chatting on the phone, speaking to a hairdresser (Pitt, 1994:13). The humour arises from the gap between the perception of social roles, codes of behaviour and appropriate registers of language in Shakespeare's world and those in our own. It is a subject to which she returns throughout her work. One of the most effective examples is 'Titania to Bottom', a revisioning of the relationship between the bewitched Fairy Queen Titania and tradesman Bottom from Shakespeare's *A Midsummer Night's Dream*. Shakespeare's Titania recoils in horror when she awakes from what she thinks of as a bad dream in which she was besotted with an ass, ('O How mine eyes do loathe his vision now!'). Fanthorpe, in her poem, interrogates this denial. Her Fairy Queen begins with a complaint, somewhat petulant, in the manner of a contemporary actress, 'You had all the best lines. I / Was the butt, too immortal / To be taken seriously' (NV:50; CP:276). She goes on to confess:

> You, Bottom, are what I love. That nose,
> Supple, aware; that muzzle, planted out
> With stiff, scratchable hairs; those ears,
> Lofty as bulrushes, smelling of hay harvest,
> Twitching to each subtle electric
> Flutter of the brain! ...
>
> ... holding you I held the whole
> Perishable world, rainfall, and nightjar,
> Tides, excrement, dandelions, the first foot,
> The last pint, high blood pressure, accident, prose.

The monologue ends with a reversal of the more familiar human yearning for immortality:

> But Bottom, Bottom,
> How I shook to the shuffle of your mortal heart.
> (CP:276)

In its sense of irreverence and fun, in its musicality, in its creation of a speaking voice, in its surprising changes of tone from the slightly grotesque to the lyrical, this has all the hallmarks of a Fanthorpe poem. Despite turning the tables, it points to a truth about *A Midsummer Night's Dream* – the fairy world is spun out of the imaginings of 'mere' mortals and it is the tension between those two spheres that captures the audience's imagination. Above all, in the poem's insistence on the significance of the mortal heart, in its acknowledgement of the reach and depth and scope and limitation of the human condition, it is a Fanthorpe poem. It displays her wit, the virtuosity with language and line, the craftsmanship for which she is well known, all those ingredients which have made her popular as a reader.

Unauthorised versions

Fanthorpe has been a tremendous ambassador for poetry, reading at venues throughout the country including the burgeoning literary festival scene, often accompanied by her long-term partner Dr Rosie Bailey, to whom all her books are dedicated and who enacts some of the many voices in her poetry in their famous 'Double Act' (captured in the Penguin audio tape of that name).

A performance for the *riverlines* series in York (15/04/04) ended with a reading of *'Deus v Adam and Another'*, in which Fanthorpe playfully imagines a Counsel for Defence summing up a case against a Mr Adam and a Mrs Eve who are accused of theft, by pointing out there is no case to answer, no evidence, and that the only witness who appears in court 'literally legless ... has been got at' (CP:329). In another 'Unauthorised Version' Fanthorpe imagines the sisterly understanding between Mary and Martha, to which Jesus, as a man, would not have had access. The work they do in the background sets the scenario for the miracles. In speaking as 'Marty's sister', Mary is defending Martha who gets a 'monumental dressing-down' from 'Josh' (i.e. Jesus) after her complaint that she's been left alone with the catering (St Luke 10 vv38-42).

> I was there; I heard what was said, and
> I knew what was meant. The men will write it up later
> From their angle, of course. But this is me, Mary,

Setting the record straight.
(WB:67; CP:238)

Fanthorpe always prefers the unauthorised version. She not only re-visions stories and images from previous generations of writers and artists, but also makes very vivid a wide gallery of characters, historical and contemporary. Some are fictitious, or constructed personae, which take their starting point in real events: in 'The Person's Tale' (VO:72; CP:177), the 'person from Porlock' who interrupted Coleridge's dream of Kubla Khan gets a chance to give his side of the story. A very different culture and social world is evoked in 'Dear Mr Lee' (WB 22; CP:202) in which we hear the voice of a failing schoolgirl, or schoolboy, writing an appreciative letter to the author Laurie Lee in one breathless sentence:

so, Dear Laurie, I want to say sorry,
I didn't want to write a character-sketch
of your mother under headings, it seemed
wrong somehow when you'd made her so lovely. (CP:202)

The extraordinariness of the ordinary

People's lives command attention when Fanthorpe reveals the extraordinariness of so called ordinary people, including neighbours, friends, and the outpatients at the psychiatric unit where she worked as a clerk, and where she began to write poetry. On the other hand, she reveals the human dimension of figures who have become legendary. She's also drawn to people of exceptional, though often unsung or under-acknowledged achievement, who live on the edge or in extreme situations; people who, despite the odds stacked against them, have followed their vocation, climbed their mountains, written their poems. Her poetry gives insights into their particular acts of faith and tenacity in adverse circumstances.

Their human dilemmas are made very present to the reader: people like Tyndale, the translator of the Bible into the vernacular, which for the first time put understanding of the scriptures into the hands of ordinary people ('Tyndale in Darkness' SAH:14; CP:296); George Fox, founder of the Quaker movement to which Fanthorpe belongs ('Fox Unearthed' C:23; CP:358); Ralph Shirley, who built the parish church at 'Staunton Harold' (C:27; CP:362) in the face of persecution which cost him his life. Mallory, who some still believe may have been the first to reach the summit before his death on Everest, is commemorated in 'On the North Face' (Q:88; CP:466). Here we have an exceptional man who is found to be a mere mortal too. Fanthorpe is responding to details in a news account of the discovery of Mallory's body:

> The Yanks who find him look like astronauts
> In their correct kit. They're not prepared for this.
> *O my Gahd! O my Gahd!* His matches.
> His unpaid Gamages' bill. His letter from home
> (The children have flu). He's one of them,
>
> For all his old world gear, his storm-bleached body.
> This is Mallory. *A modern person.* A man they know.
> (CP:466)

Fanthorpe ends the poem by replacing the 'jaunty psalm' they sang with a quotation from *The Tibetan Book of the Dead*: 'O ye compassionate ones, defend Mallory, / Who is defenceless. Protect him / Who is unprotected.' She adds to this a reminder of the final glimpse of Mallory, 'Who was last seen / *Going strong for the top*' a quoted phrase which takes on new resonances at the end of the poem and reinstates a sense of Mallory alive with energy and vision. Here, as elsewhere in Fanthorpe's writing, two different worlds meet. Her poetry illuminates these moments of encounter and the cultural contexts and values against which lives, ancient and modern, are played out.

Where did this subversive streak come from, the desire to discover the unauthorised version, to speak for the silent, to value the underdog?

Early Life

Born in 1929 in Kent, Ursula Askham Fanthorpe, is the daughter of barrister Judge Richard Fanthorpe. It is perhaps to her father she owes 'the need to rectify, to correct the balance' when she feels things are unfair 'especially perhaps on the part of the dispossessed' (Wainwright, 1995:70). As children she and her brother were cast in roles as counsel for the defence and prosecution, and became aware early of the need for adequate evidence or witness to support their case. The construction of herself as a watcher and witness will be the subject of the second chapter of this study.

Being the daughter of a judge created a materially comfortable childhood. But her poems testify to a degree of discomfort engendered by the awareness that the arrival of children had meant the end of her mother's promising career in the civil service, and that as a child she somehow fell short of expectations:

> She had a dancer's feet, elegant witty.
> We had our father's, maverick spreaders of dirt. (C:31; CP:366)

Fanthorpe's mother, whose ancestors can be traced back to Roger Askham, tutor to Elizabeth I, had a passion for drama and opera, particularly the works of Gilbert and Sullivan. This sense of drama and love of music was passed on to her daughter who also records that one of the few positive things from her schooling was the importance of her introduction to choral music and the understanding that it is based however tenuously on words – 'Music I suddenly saw could speak' (in ASLH).

Fanthorpe found it hard to forgive her parents the choice of Christian name, Ursula, which translates as 'little female bear'. As her cleaner comments so forthrightly, in her Bristol dialect, *'thassa funny name you got. Latin ennit? I'm Olive'* (C:68; CP:396). (It is this same cleaner she imagines as the ideal reader of her poems.) The embarrassment of this name was mitigated slightly when, as a child reader, her father gave her a copy of *Quo Vadis*, a novel by the Polish writer Sienkowicz. She became acquainted with Ursus the gigantic faithful retainer who excelled at killing with a single blow. At this stage of her life, with a typical teenager's anxiety about body image and a mistaken sense of being gigantic, she comments with characteristic self irony:

> I became him; loyal, colossal, taciturn, *dangerous*. I lived a happy fantasy life, rescuing my parents, off-handedly eliminating girls I didn't like at school ... towering over everyone else.
> (*Autobiography of a Reader*)

The very conscious decision to publish under initials was not simply to do with this dislike of a name. She saw it as an opportunity to reinvent herself and is known as U.A. to most of her friends and readers. It also deliberately disguised gender as she was well aware of the difference of treatment meted out to male and female poets by the predominantly male critics when she first began publishing in the late 1970's. The critical reception of women's poetry is in fact still an issue in the early twenty-first century.

Awareness of gender inequality was perceived quite early in childhood as she records in the poem 'Kinch and Lack'. There is clearly an early anger, a sense of injustice that she lives at a time when the boy in the family is the one to benefit from preparatory school education, though she is 'two years older, / Taller [has] read more books' (C:30; CP:365). Here her brother is being measured for a uniform, and the poet remembers how, as a child, she absorbed something of the ritual significance of this. She explores her intimations of the complexities of her mother's feelings on this rite of passage, as well as her own realisation as a young girl, that 'there's a world enlisting him / That hasn't a place for me.' This epiphany leads to a statement of both acceptance and resistance. 'O.K. I'll make my own' (CP:366). She has acknowledged an early ambition to be a writer, though she didn't initially imagine herself as a poet.

The same sense of resistance to limited expectations and assumptions is voiced in 'The Benefactors' (Q:69; CP:456). She thanks all those who poured cold water on her initiatives and achievements; those who asked her parents, *'Why waste money / On educating a daughter?'* Those who considered she'd *'do better to stay at home, learning / To be the wife of some good man.'* Those who provided a chorus, *'Oh no! / Not at your age / You'll live to regret it / I wouldn't if I were you.'* In a bleakly ironic acknowledgement she ends her poem, 'Without your help, I'd never have brought it off' (CP:456).

The more serious threat to her early welfare, however, was the impact of the Second World War. She writes very movingly and graphically in 'Sirensong' (SAH:2; CP307) of the shock of the experience of those war time raids on her Kent home town of Bromley. Fanthorpe re-imagines the solidity and texture of her childhood home in this poem from the ironically titled *Safe as Houses* (1995). She recalls how her 'baby knees crawled through it, certain of polished parquet, / Turkey carpets, quarry-tiled kitchen floor./ My knees understood this was a forever house' (CP:308). But all those certainties were overturned as she came to know how 'bombs sliced off a house's flank / Uncovering private parts'. The air raids spelt 'the end of faith in brick'; the end of innocence, of childhood. The shock of seeing what was once so solid and certain turn to rubble made a lasting impression.

She would be nine at this point when London was undergoing bombing raids and children were evacuated to safer areas. When war broke out her school simply closed and her parents were advised to evacuate her to a boarding school in Surrey, which was conveniently only five miles away from her brother's relocated school, which enabled them to visit both children in the same weekend. Despite the geographic closeness, U.A. was only able to see her brother when her parents made this journey. The knowledge of the wartime anxieties already faced by her parents, made it impossible for her to report home about the miseries of exile, being 'ill-fed, cold, neglected'. It was here that she began to construct herself as an outsider, joining the class three weeks into term when friendship groups had already been established. And, as she acknowledges, 'to write is the characteristic activity of the outsider' (ASLH). She has, over recent years, been working on a sequence of poems about these wartime experiences called 'The Duration'.

It was also at this stage of her life that she was, 'laying the foundations of the lifelong habit of non-conformity; of insisting on finding out for herself, of never believing what she was told by authority' (ASLH). In a later essay, 'War, Poetry the Child', Fanthorpe refers to the years from 9-18 as 'nine years of solitary dissidence' (in Hebert and Hollis, 2000:209). The reading of literature, history, myth, became in these circumstances an escape and a comfort. In her 'Autobiography of a Reader' she tells how she discovered, in her clandestine visits to the school library, the gory bits of Shakespeare, which she loved. She also tells how her heroes were Richard II 'for being different and not trying to hide it' and Coriolanus whose bold, "I banish you" to the Romans who were banishing him, stirred in her an equally resistant spirit. She had already encountered the world of *Lorna Doone*, where she 'side-stepped the author's intentions and became an enthusiastic recruit to the wrong side,' a secret Doone, riding with the band as they went out pillaging.

She later admits in her poem 'A Wartime Education' (WB:29; CP:208) that she found it hard to remember which side she was on:

Struggling through adolescence, trying
to accommodate Macbeth, parents, God,
Teachers of mathematics, it was hard
To sustain plain hatred for *The Hun*
...
Might he not, like Aeneas, have reasons
(Insufficient, but understandable) for what he did? (CP208-9)

Both the bombings and the evacuation to Surrey left their mark on Fanthorpe. 'All schools [in Bromley] were closed instantly. I never saw any of my friends again. I somehow never found compensation for this sudden and utter loss' (WPC:209). The sense of the precariousness of everything most valued, of family, of England, of life itself was indelibly etched. She explains in 'Sirensong', the consequences of war, how, 'some children are invaded forever, will never learn to be young' (SH:26; CP:308).

Despite this pervasive sense of loss, she was also an early recruit to the value of laughter as a strategy for both survival and subversion. She understands, 'the vital importance of wit, jokes, puns, anything that questions the status quo, or merely throws its own eccentric slant on life' (ASLH). Her poem 'Women Laughing' (V0:36; CP:153), a reprise of Shakespeare's Seven Ages of Man, typifies each stage of a woman's life by the kind of laughter it evokes. Its opening stanza significantly provides a preface of 'Gurgles, genderless, / Inside the incurious womb.' Each subsequent stanza moves on a stage from babyhood to girlhood, through adolescence to young womanhood, by which point even their laughter is 'anxious to please'. As wives and mothers the laughter is socially produced to encourage their men and children. Only as 'Old women, unmanned, free / Of children, embarrassment, desire to please,' does she hear them 'Hooting grossly, without explanation' (CP:153). With a very light touch, in a minimal structure, Fanthorpe has sketched in a whole pattern of the acculturation of women in our society to their prescribed roles.

In 'Growing Up' the stanzas disclose her own discomfort with the early stages of her life, 'I wasn't good / At being a baby ... / At being a child ... / At adolescence ... / At growing up / ... Conversation / Disintegrated as I touched it, / So I played mute' (VO 50-1; CP:161-2). This poem is appended as a postscript to an autobiographical piece in a collection of lesbian feminist studies, *Volcanoes and Pearl Divers,* edited by Suzanne Raitt. Fanthorpe comments that 'this poem comes closer to revelation than anything else I've written,' (Raitt1995:11). The poem records a sense of awkwardness of growing up female, of being 'caught bloody-thighed, a criminal / Guilty of puberty' (CP:161). As if to be female in itself is to be strange, to be different. There is the added complication and awkwardness explained in the essay of the realisation during this period of confusion about her sexual identity, another significant element in her sense of outsiderness. She explains. 'I couldn't start [writing] until I knew who or where I was' (Raitt, 1995:10) and that came much later. 'Growing Up' paradoxically affords articulate insights into the difficulty of self-understanding and self-expression at these early stages of her life. The quality of silence and the expressive muteness of others is something she returns to again and again once she has found her voice as a poet.

Even when she went on to study language and literature at St Anne's College Oxford where she gained a First in English, Fanthorpe still felt on the periphery of things. Constant reminders during the war that 'careless talk costs lives' had 'encouraged a habit of taciturnity' (WPC:208), a sense that it was unsafe to speak one's feelings aloud. In an autobiographical piece called 'Slow Learner' she revealed that at university she felt herself to be 'callow' compared with the many ex-servicemen and women who were finishing off degrees that war had interrupted. She perceived them as 'redolent with Experience' and 'naturally more interesting to the tutors than my generation could be' (SL). She again felt muffled, unsure of what she had to contribute.

It wasn't until many years later, after leaving her job as Head of English at Cheltenham Ladies College, where she had taught for 16 years, that she really found a subject and a voice. Fanthorpe first talks about this move in 'Slow Learner'. She had assumed that a writer needed experience, that experience meant people, that schools were full of people therefore teaching would be a good route to follow:

> Sixteen years later I awoke from academic slumber and realised that sixteen years' growth of pupils had gone on to find experience, lived among people and generally done things that I'd wanted to, while I had contented myself with working to free them. (SL:35)

The glass dugout

Fanthorpe eventually 'disentangled [herself] from pupils, the Burnham Scale and the bicycle shed mentality,' and after doing a counselling course, a brief period on the dole, then working as a *temp*, she finally found a job as a clerk / receptionist at the Burden Institute, the neuro-psychiatric unit at Frenchay Hospital, Bristol. She had previously experienced from a patient's point of view the fascination with the closed world of a hospital when, as a result of a traffic accident, she'd had to spend three months in the the Radcliffe Infirmary. It left her with a desire to swap careers and go into nursing; a desire squashed by her parents and tutors. The neuro-psychiatric unit was a very different sort of hospital. It was here, whilst organising outpatient clinics, she says that 'poetry happened to her.'

In an interview with Carole Baldock she explains, 'I began writing because I was angry and there was no-one there to listen to me being angry' (1999:9). The anger was in part at the way the bureaucracy of the hospital expected her to deal with patients, and in part at the way doctors reserved a different language for them. In 'Hospitalspeak' (H), which she refers to as 'an account of rebellion against the hospital's officially reasonable outlook', Fanthorpe remembers her particular outrage at the way patients were deprived of their dignity, 'by allowing them only weasel verbs. For one doctor, patients never *said* anything: they *claimed, admitted, denied*' (H:31). The 'glass dugout' is Fanthorpe's phrase for her observation point in the hospital:

> I feel as if I am in a forward zone or a trench. I am a lay person in a professional world, and because of this I am invisible, not really there. That's very akin to the common soldier. ... You are exposed to extremes, and you have to be ready in the same sort of way as a soldier. I think they call it "standing-to". (Interview with Diana Hendry, 1985)

This military metaphor, with which she validates her right to write, provides the title of her 1982 volume *Standing To* but is echoed frequently throughout her work. She conveys a clear sense of being caught in the crossfire between the official demands of her own situation as receptionist / clerk and the unofficial demands of the patients on her as a human being with deeply held Christian beliefs and a writer's sensibility. The projected voice of the hospital authority is heard in 'Jobdescription: Medical Records' 'We do not encourage speculation in clerks' (SE:12; CP:24). The more this voice outlines the requirements of the position, 'We prefer you / To think of patients not as people, but / Digits ... Our system / Is terminal digit filing ... /... You will use / The Death Book as a matter of routine' (CP:24), the more evident becomes the tension between Fanthorpe the clerk and Fanthorpe the human being. Out of this tension the early poetry arises. She became attentive to the qualities of these brain-damaged, confused patients and their relatives and concerned at her own powerlessness to help. She admired their 'stoicism, their cheerfulness, their patience' (SL). 'The List', which opens her first collection, shows her awareness of the discrepancy between the surface order and dignity she can confer through her 'flawlessly typed' list on which the names, 'spaced / At the proper intervals, / serene and lordly' appear 'like giftbearers on a frieze', and the actuality:

> Tomorrow these names will turn nasty,
> Senile, pregnant, late,
> Handicapped, handcuffed, unhandy,
> Muddled, moribund, mute,
>
> Be stained by living. (SE:9; CP:21)

This use of an alliterative list with its emphatic rhythms, its assonances and semantic linkages and carefully orchestrated half rhymes, has become a hallmark of Fanthorpe's wordplay.

Fanthorpe wrote 'for and about the voiceless; the patients, the cleaning ladies' (SL). She felt she was 'doing something not only to redress the way patients are spoken of in case notes', but also to 'celebrate the tremendous energy and resourcefulness of their ways with words' (H). Her two 'Casehistory' poems are as far removed from the official medical case history format and language as possible. Both are very poignant portraits of young women who, through illness or injury, stand in a problematic relationship with their former selves. Julie who suffers from encephalitis asks:

> I'm not mental am I?
> Someone told me I was mental,
> But I lost my memory
> 'Cos our dad died.
> It don't make sense though do it?
> After I've been a nurse. (SE:18; CP:25-6)

Stanzas like this are 'found' poems in that they take the phrases and rhythms and dialect forms of the woman's actual speech. They are prefaced by four lines of Fanthorpe's own which economically select details to make Julie vivid and very present to the reader:

> She stands between us. Her dress
> Is zipped up back to front.
> She has been crying her eyes
> Dark. Her legs are thinner than legs. (CP:25)

Julie's monologue is punctuated by lines borrowed from *Hamlet*, descriptive of Ophelia's madness, lyrical words resonant with loss and pathos. In this new context they frame Julie's utterances and raise her to an equally tragic status.

The poet imagines the internal monologue of the subject of another 'Casehistory: Alison (head injury)'. The poem opens as the patient looks at a photograph of an earlier self from whom she realises she is estranged:

> I would like to have known
> My husband's wife, my mother's only daughter.
> A bright girl she was. (SE:20; CP:27)

The phrasing alerts the reader not only to Alison's tragedy but the impact of her accident on those close to her. There are other unheard monologues hovering behind the one presented.

The speaker of the poem is aware of the physical and mental changes that her accident has caused. 'Enmeshed in comforting / Fat, I wonder at her delicate angles'. The brain-damaged Alison looks at an Alison in the photograph who 'knows my father's dead', 'has digested / mourning,' whereas, 'I who need reminding / Every morning, shall never get over what / I do not remember.' The monologue ends with the one piece of knowledge that is particular to the injured Alison:

> I know
> For all my damaged brain, something she doesn't:
> I am her future.
>
> A bright girl she was. (CP:28)

There is something about the placing of the line endings, the spaces in the poems, that lets the full weight of these lines find their maximum charge. So Fanthorpe fleshes out the statistics and lets the reader's imagination encompass the full emotional and psychological implications of the diagnostic labels which form the titles of these two poems.

The tension in her own position becomes more explicit in the later poem 'Clerical Error' (NV:15; CP:250). The persona here seems to be charged with a crime and is addressing her mitigating circumstances to a 'you', a 'Sir', who is not her immediate boss at the hospital, but a higher authority. The clerical error is not simply a flaw in the typing, but more significantly the tone she takes with the patients when under stress:

> What must I do when Job and his daughters
>
> Cram into my office where they are not allowed.
>
> I address them as *love*
> (which is an insult) , and say in a special soothing voice
> (which fools no one) *Go to the nurses, Judith,*

Judith, the nurses are looking for you (which is a lie).
(CP:250-1)

She is aware that she is living with two conflicting sets of commandments here. One is to get the medical records typed 'against the clock'; the other to attend to the afflicted and the poor. The poem is the only site of reconciliation.

In a later poem, entitled 'Back to the Front' (NV:12; CP:248) she returns to find the office changed and feels threatened by its 'new toys, compact, intense, / User-unfriendly.' The patients 'still huddle and fumble, and somewhere / Someone is still screaming.' But more disturbing is the assumption by one of her former colleagues that she *'would have enjoyed yesterday'*. They think she would have relished 'Laura's language / *Words Averil had never heard before ... We had to explain them.*' Shocked, she asks herself:

> Would I ever have enjoyed yesterday? Was I,
> Before I went away, so good at relishing
> The anger of the helpless, such an eavesdropper
> On misery? I suppose I was. I suppose that
> Was how I lived, semi-attached to despair. (CP:249)

In her earlier poem 'Patients', Fanthorpe had drawn a distinction, not between the sick and the well, but between the diagnosed and the undiagnosed, which includes herself. She exposes the strange idiosyncrasies of those who pass for normal. Paul Delaney (1998:5) notes: 'Fanthorpe offers an oblique ray of light that reveals we've been peering through a window that turns out to be a mirror'.

Credo Arts Community gave a multi-media presentation based on a selection of U.A.Fanthorpe's poems (initially for Hull Literature Festival in 1998 and revived for *riverlines* in York, March 2003) in a piece called *Self-Assembly*. They used choreography, puppets, masks, mime and projections of documentary archive with orchestrated readings of the poems arranged along a narrative time line from the cradle to the grave. This performance embodied the same critical insight as Delaney's about the double-edged reflectiveness in Fanthorpe's poetry when the cards held by the chorus line were suddenly flipped over to be revealed as mirrors which were shone at and reflected the audience. Observation and witness is a complex process at the heart of Fanthorpe's poetry that reveals as much about the observer as the observed. Her poetry uses strategies to disconcertingly disrupt her own and the reader's viewpoint, to help question our ways of looking and being in the world, to remind us of our connection with the lives under scrutiny, of the potential, the responsibility and the fragility of being human.

Chapter Two

Acts of attention and translation

If I have any objective, it's to bear witness, to say, "I have seen this, and no one else was there looking at that precise moment"; especially perhaps on behalf of the dispossessed.

(Wainwright, 1995:70)

It is not surprising, given the influence of her lawyer father, that Fanthorpe sees her role as a poet 'to be a witness' and understands that 'the responsibility of the witness is to speak out' (Baldock, 1999:9). This chapter will explore not only her own acts of attention to the world around her through the medium of words and poetic form, but also her fascination with artists and their medium of line and colour, their acts of translating observed experience on to paper or canvas.

The comment in the epigraph was made initially in the context of her work in the hospital, where she was in a position to gain insight into a world she hadn't imagined, and which she felt would be unknown to most of her readers, 'a world of the epileptic, the depressed, the brain-damaged, the violent, the helpless' (SL:67). She also wanted to bear witness to the stoicism of the patients' families and visitors. 'I wanted to testify to the way they went on being human in the midst of such confusion' (H:33). This need to testify seems to give permission to speak out for a poet who earlier had expressed her feeling of being silenced, muffled, mute. The people she previously thought had experience worth talking about were the soldiers who fought in the Second World War and it is significant that the metaphors she uses to describe her situation as a receptionist are predominantly military:

> [The patients] seemed like World War 1 casualties staggering through No Man's Land while I watched from the safety of my dugout (H:33).

Fanthorpe explains in her essay, 'War, Poetry, The Child', that she found her voice 'among the sad little individual wars of a neuro-psychiatric hospital ... the distress I encountered there seemed to liberate my vocation' (WPC:210).

It was in a very early poem, 'The Watcher' (omitted from *Selected Poems* 1986 but reinstated in *Collected Poems* 2005) where she first constructed this persona of observer for herself:

> I am a watcher; and the things I watch
> Are birds and love.   (SE:10; CP:22)

This is immediately qualified by, 'Not the more common sorts of either kind.' Not 'young couples ... blessed by church and state' but 'quiet lovers, miles from wedding bells ... / Finding their nesting places in hospitals and prison cells.' It is perhaps one of the first acknowledgements in her poetry, though oblique, of her own sexuality and awareness of difference. This could also contribute to her sense of outsiderness. She has herself suggested that:

> Possibly there is some connection between my homosexuality and my inclination to watch people or write about them as if I were non-existent, or a fly on the wall (Raitt, 1995:10).

Hence her empathy with the human equivalents of 'the rare Welsh kite, /... The tiny wren / ... and the nightingale, / Chased from her home by bulldozers and speculating men' (CP:22). These breeds, the rare and the marginal are what attract her interest. She draws our attention here to two different motives of speculation – wonder and profit. She has nothing but scorn for the speculators and looks with compassion on their victims. Poet and ornithologist share an attention to detail. Carol Rumens has said that all poetry is close-looking, whether inward at emotional reality or outward at the world. There is perhaps a subtle difference between being a watcher and being a witness. Watching could be a passive or silent occupation whereas witnessing involves speaking out, being counted, acknowledging that words have consequences.

Truth is hard to translate

That sense of a calling to witness the world and especially to record the otherwise disregarded is reflected in the titles of many of her early volumes, *Side Effects* (1978), *Standing To* (1982), *Voices Off* (1984). The title of her 1987 collection *A Watching Brief* links this sense of vocation as a writer with the work done by visual artists and also points to the legal implications of witness. This link is carried through into her more recent work. *Consequences* (2000) reflects on the consequences of choices made by individuals and nations, and particularly for the poet the choice of words. Her poem 'The Witness' from this collection is the most explicit at voicing the tension between the need to witness, to be a truth teller, and the impossibility of giving evidence that is sufficiently accurate, impartial, meaningful. In this poem, which alludes to a scene from Dostoyevsky's *Crime and Punishment*, with the accused in the dock 'picturesque as Raskolnikov', the notion of witness and outsider are brought together when, in the courtroom scene, Fanthorpe shifts the focus from the key players to the unnamed witness:

> Let us now

> Examine the witness. He is the outsider,
> He belongs to another court, pursuing
> A different code. He is messenger
> Of what happened, expert without diploma,
> Suspect as a prisoner, innocent as a judge.

> All he can say is what he saw,
> And that's an old story. Cross-examined,
> He flounders. His vigilance is fishy,
> His ignorance shady. Truth is hard to translate
> When our only machinery is words.
> (C:62; CP:391-2)

When Fanthorpe has proclaimed so many times her own role as witness, it is hard not to see this poem as reflecting the author's own doubts about the limitations of a mere mortal to achieve the role she has set for herself. The plural pronoun 'our' seems to conflate the subject of observation with the poet and the reader.

No observing eye is innocent and it is interesting to see to which subjects Fanthorpe directs our attention, and how she becomes increasingly aware of and articulate about the problems the artist, the poet and the ordinary man or woman in the street face in translating what is seen and felt into language, into utterance, or marks on the page. What she is a witness to, as much as anything, is the very problem of truth telling.

In 'Soothing and Awful', a poem that recalls Larkin's 'Church Going', Fanthorpe examines the remarks put in the visitors' book at Montacute Church in Somerset (CP:158-9). The poem begins with her realisation that 'You are meant to exclaim. The Church / Expects it of you.' The abruptness of this opening statement indicates alarm: what can be said? The whole business of the convention of a visitors' book, of expressing a response to the experience of seeing the church is interrogated here. Browsing through the 'cosys' and 'nices' she reads between the lines to see how even here the choice of phrase and style of handwriting inevitably reveal something about the authors, 'Someone from Dudley, whose writing suggests tight shoes / Reported *Nice and Cool*. The young entry / Yelp their staccato approval: / *Super! Fantastic! Jesus Lives! Ace!*' (CP:159). Faced with the same task (and the same limited space) she recognises how hard it is for any, including herself, to express meaningfully just what it is that is experienced on such occasions. Could she in fact do any better than the interesting paradox, '*Soothing and Awful*', of the entry chosen for the title?

> But what they found,
> Whatever it was, it wasn't what
> They say. In the beginning,
>
> We know, the word, but not here,
> Land of the perpetually flowering cliché,
> The rigid lip. (VO:46; CP:158)

At this point in the poem there is a move from third to first person plural as she considers the contribution of ancestors to the Church, 'our fathers who piled / Stone upon stone, our mothers / Who stitched hassocks, our cousins / Whose bones lie smooth, harmonious around.' This move joins author and reader into a common sense of heritance and belonging. There may of course be resistant readers, but England for a long time was built around parishes where the Church was the centre of each community. The subtle shift from the patriarchal language of the Lord's Prayer, 'Our Father', to the more domestic plural 'our fathers / mothers / cousins', acknowledges the church is the body of believers, including the unnamed women, and workers. That shift is prompting the same sort of questions as Brecht's, 'A Worker Reads and Asks': 'Who built Thebes in Seven Days? / Books say it was Kings'. Unlike Larkin, Fanthorpe steps into this church as a Christian, but she is not an unquestioning reader of the scriptures. The final line of her poem includes not only the reader but the poet too in the common problem of finding a language adequate to express the experience:

> However majestic their gifts, comely their living,
> Their words would be thin like ours; they would join
> In our inarticulate anthem: *Very Cosy.*   (VO:47; CP:159)

Paradoxically, in taking the space of a whole poem to explore the complex feelings triggered by the short blank space in the visitors' book, she has managed to convey vivid details about her visit and also her reflections on the differences and links between the world which built the Church and the world in which it is now often just part of our heritage industry. Fanthorpe has been extremely articulate in voicing her anxieties on the subject of self-expression.

Another poem which looks at somewhat formulaic writing, produced under the pressure of limited space, is 'Postcards'. She approaches them initially through the eyes of the postman who 'studies his handful / Before he slots them home.'

> Public as T-shirts, coded like
> A mole's correspondence, designed to be enigmatic.
> (C:59-60; CP:389)

She imagines him puzzled not only by the clichés: '*Having a wonderful ... Oh boy / This is the life! ... Had to put / Our cardies on ... Wish you were here*', but puzzled also by the choice of images, 'Fish;

teapots; *eucryphia milleganii* / (What'll she make of that? he thinks popping it in)' (CP:389-90).

The poem then changes in tone, moves from couplets to tercets, as the author addresses the postman and implicitly the reader, urging him to:

> Look in the graveyard, as you make your rounds;
> There are the ultimate postcards, trite as ever,
> Stylised as runes, with a subtext intricate
>
> As a crossword puzzle clue, or house-agent's blurb,
> Delivering the last message of stay-at-homes
> To those who have left on a journey beyond deliveries:
>
> *Gone, not forgotten; Sadly missed; Wish you were here.*
> (C:60; CP:390)

The poem draws attention to the complexities of the meanings of texts for intended and unintended audiences. The poignancy lies in the impossibility of finding a short phrase adequate to the expression of loss and the fact that the dead for whom the message is really intended can no longer receive their 'postcards'. What are these words really about other than the desire to communicate beyond the grave?

How can experiential material be turned into black and white code, and how as readers do we lift a sense of three dimensional experience from two dimensional marks? The processes for the writer and artist are seen as beyond the rational. The poem 'In Residence', for fellow writer Anita Mason, describes something of the concentration needed and the mystery involved in the process:

> Watcher by the wordhoard, waiting
> Alone for the lightning, the long night
> When the patterns show plain as parsley
> And pen knows its way along the paper. (WB:45; CP:223)

I was set here to watch

This sense of witness appears in a wide range of contexts throughout Fanthorpe's work. Difficult though communication is, it has to be attempted. The title poem of her 1982 collection *Standing To* is voiced by a persona who comments:

> This is turning into a long war.
> I must have been mobilised
> In the womb ...

What war is being talked about is left somewhat ambiguous:

> The enemy is not
> The one who declares war,
> Who is as mortal as you.
>
> The true enemy declares
> Nothing, cannot be disposed of,
> Is never indisposed.
>
> I was set here
> To watch. So I do. (S T:94; CP:128)

Just what war is this, where the speaker has to 'report in cipher, to headquarters, / Which is an hypothesis', and asks:

> Are there others recruited
> Like me, encoding what they see,
> Abandoned by Higher Command,
> Unable to desert?

What is this calling that is being doubted? A calling to poetry? A calling to God? A mixture of the two? It is not an easy task to be called, as she illustrates in 'Getting it Across', one of several poems where Fanthorpe enacts the problem of a character struggling to communicate, most dramatically here through the assumed persona of Christ in his attempts at 'getting it across' to his disciples:

I envy Moses, who could choose
The diuturnity of stone for waymarks ...

I alone must write on flesh ...

I am tattooing God on their makeshift lives.   (ST:71; CP:109)

He has to construe their frowns, their 'jaw cracking yawns' as he comes out with one of his 'old chestnuts'. He imagines their responses in their own Billingsgate vernacular:

... Christ! Not that bloody
Sower again, they are saying, or God!
Not the prodigal bleeding son.
Give us a new one for Messiah's sake.   (ST:70; CP108)

Fanthorpe has Christ realise they are 'unfitted for ... analogy,' that his 'sheep and goats, / Virgins, pigs, fig trees, loaves and lepers / Confuse them.' Fanthorpe's analogies for the disciples shift dramatically in the final verse: one minute they are envisioned (by Christ) as 'Keystone Cops ... Running absurdly away, or lying ineptly, / Cutting off ears and falling into the water'; the next they are:

Sancho Panzas ...
Dying ridiculous and undignified,
Flayed and stoned and crucified upside down.
They are the dear, the human, the dense, for whom
My message is. That might, had I not touched them,
Have died decent respectable upright deaths in bed.
(ST:70; CP109)

Being a disciple is a privilege, but it exacts a harsh penalty. Jesus has to get the message across so it can be relayed after him. But words are difficult things. As a receptionist Fanthorpe realised she also was a translator, 'explaining the demotic of patient and doctor ... In all this hurly-burly of codes and languages I discovered I had my own' (H:33).

Her own code is of course poetry, and she seeks in this medium to find how best to harness her own powers with words to do what little she can in the face of the dilemmas presented. Stylistically, while adept at formal metres and fixed forms, she comments, 'there was a point, somewhere in the middle of *Standing To*, when I saw I'd get where I wanted to be by *breaking* the rules' (Wainwright, 1995:74).

In an early poem, 'Patience Strong', Fanthorpe draws a distinction between the clichéd sentiments 'in homespun verse / Disguised as prose,' and genuine poets whose message is more oblique, 'doesn't fit / A pocket diary's page.' The poem's first stanza adopts a tone dismissive of Patience Strong:

> Her theme
> Always the same: rain falls in every life,
> But rainbows, bluebirds, spring, babies or God
> Lift up our hearts. No doubt such rubbish sells. (SE:22; CP:28)

The second stanza turns its attention to an epileptic out-patient. In the simplest of details she records the story of this encounter:

> One day, in epileptic outpatients,
> A working man, a fellow in his fifties,
> Was feeling bad. I brought a cup of tea.
> He talked about his family and job:
> His dad was in the Ambulance Brigade;
> He hoped to join, but being epileptic,
> They wouldn't have him. *Naturally*, he said,
> *With my disease, I'd be a handicap,*
> *But I'd have liked to help.* (CP:29)

What could be less oblique than this? What more powerful poetry than the unassuming words of this patient? That one word *naturally* says so much about the shared assumptions of the time about disability and his acceptance of that view. His words are the real power of the poem, yet he turns from the genuine comfort of a real listener to unwrap 'from some special inner pocket, / A booklet muffled up in cellophane.' The poet glimpses the characteristic features of Patience Strong's work, the 'cottage garden ... chintzy casement windows.'

And *See*, he said, *this is what keeps me going.* (CP:29)

This in a way is a twofold rebuff. It fails to acknowledge her concern to help in a role as receptionist, and also is a slap in the face for her view of real poetry.

The poem has observed all sorts of acts of communication and empathy, but in turning the tables on her own dismissive stance, undermining the previous certainties, it also reveals something of the mystery of the way the world of words and poetry in particular communicates and resonates with individual readers.

In the beginning were the words

The means and process of translating what is seen and understood into marks on paper, whether these are made by words or paint also fascinates. 'In the beginning were the words,' as she reminds us in the opening line of her poem 'Genesis', written for the author J.R.R.Tolkien, a former tutor:

Aristocratic, cryptic, chromatic.
Vowels as direct as midday,
Consonants lanky as long-swords. (ST:74; CP:112)

She, like Larkin, is aware that 'words as plain as hen-birds' wings / Do not lie, / Do not overbroider things,' (Larkin, 1988:26) and she shows a preference for the Anglo Saxon which expresses itself in 'Words for Months':

Their names in this country
Wore out, though the weather
Is still what they charted:

They fit better, the dull
Words for difficult things:
Mud. Milk. Weeds. Leaf-fall. Cull. (C:33; CP:367-8)

Fanthorpe is fascinated by etymology. Speaking in the voice of 'The Vulgar Tongue' she comments:

I am old, weather-beaten, subtle.
Invasion and invention have taught me
Not to be surprised by anything. (Q:27; CP:432)

In 'Caedmon's Song' (CP:433) she goes back to the Old English version of this hymn and presents it in a modern Tyneside idiom:

Forst there was nowt   nowt and neewhere
God felt the empty   space wi his finga
Let's hev sum   light sez God
Ootbye and inbye   so the light happened

What happens to our understanding of this central story of creation when it is transposed from its weighty Old English form into a local dialect? We get a different feel of the nature of God, somehow more homely. The terms 'ootbye and inbye' are idiomatic directional instructions that a Northumbrian farmer would call to his dogs. It seems as if the light is being herded in by two faithful sheepdogs and the image of God the shepherd is invoked in the process. Fanthorpe's poetry alerts us to subtleties of language use, shifts over time, differences of dialect and jargon, but also to the innate weight and rhythm of words ... their textures, particular mixes of vowels and consonants. Words are there to be savoured.

In fact the whole business of print is there to be savoured too as she records in 'Colophon' (SAH:55; CP:332). A trip to Slough with her partner, Rosie, to buy a small flatbed press as advertised in

Exchange and Mart, presents them with a whole array of redundant presses, 'Great gaunt things loom around ... / Hoping for work.' These speak to Fanthorpe about the power of the first output of the presses 'whose work was burned, / Chained, or inherited, precious as manors' and the skills of the printers and journeymen who worked them, a whole way of life and set of values felt as 'a great gape of loss, like losing one's language' (CP:333). The poem is a riposte to a quotation from Peter Kindersley of Dorling Kindersley that serves as the poem's epigraph:

> 'We're not going out of the book business, we're just throwing away the paper and print ... Books won't disappear. They'll just become marginalised.'

The sensibilities of the vendor, the 'Man / In overalls, cloth-capped; a Berkshire voice' are also celebrated here. A man who can appreciate '*Perpetua. Lovely Perpetua*' as he shows them the old fonts. A man whose final raised hand on their departure is read as a blessing. The need for print, for books is something to which she returns in the final poem of her *Collected Poems 1978-2003*, 'Libraries at War'. She remembers the 'pinched economy / Utility war-time things, their coarse paper, their frail covers' which none-theless encapsulated 'such brightness in the dark.'

> The more you destroy them, the louder we call. (Q:85;CP:468)

This sentiment is one re-echoed by Marina Warner in a recent lecture to Friends of the Bodleian Library (edited version in *Guardian Review* 06/08/05 p.22) where she emphasises the import-ance of the material presence of books. She had brought a special Enitharmon edition of Heaney's *Testament of Cresseid* (after the Scottish poet Henryson) into her seminar: 'the book's material presence changed our relationship to the poem and imprinted it more richly in memory.' It is not the same as working from a photocopy or reading online.

The records are riddles

From early childhood Fanthorpe is aware both of the material presence of texts, and also that texts, both spoken and written, have to be deciphered, whether it be 'the churchbells / With their nightly riddles', or the Vikings' stone inscriptions:

> The records are riddles, chiselled in
> Angular runes, hard letters for stone
> Or bone, nothing so lax as parchment. (VO:28; CP:147)

Here something of the import is understood simply from textures and materials. Sounds, she also realised, have a subtext. In 'Sounds and Silences' Fanthorpe remembers the difficulty in making sense of 'sounds heard only in childhood':

> Interminable mumbling like rock-doves
>
> Over early morning tea, after last night's differences,
> Of parents in their bedroom, creating today. (AWB:28; CP:207)

Similarly in 'Sirensong' she recalls the sounds of the air raid warning sirens:

> I know the song they sang. I heard it,
> The husky warbling, on the war's first day.
> Learned the meaning too: Lie low, lie low. (SAH:26; CP:307)

The opening line there is a response to Sir Thomas Browne's 'Urne Buriall', quoted in the epigraph, which asks 'What song the Syrens sang?' The more soothing 'voices off' in life are celebrated in 'Against Speech'; the 'Chat of World Service ... / Nurses checking ... / Parents talking things over' knowing each of these 'Signals *All's well; all's well; so far, all's well*' (C:32; CP:367).

Fanthorpe constantly emphasises the process of understanding the world, of constructing meaning and insight from sounds, words, gestures, signs, brushstrokes. Even place names have a history, are interrogated and enriched. In 'Strong Language in South Gloucestershire'(C:34; CP:369) she explores the life of local place names, 'names / Tough and diehard as crypts'. She thinks back to their inception: 'No committee okayed them. They happened, like grass, / Written down all anyhow / By cosmopolitan clerks in a hurry. / Ramshackle riddles' (CP:369). She then reflects on their current life as utterance, 'their proper stresses a password / Known only to cautious locals,' and also notes their manifestations as road signs, 'inscribed in steel'. The poem ends by revealing their etymology; they are 'still proclaiming / Here are Soppa's tinpot two acres, / Something holy, a good place for blackbirds, / Duck farm, bridge over mud, / The stranger's bright city.' The footnote reveals the places referred to are 'various Sodburys; Nympsfield; Ozleworth; Doughton; Slimbridge; Gloucester' (CP:369).

This fascination with names was explored in a much earlier poem, 'On Buying OS Sheet 163'. This is the Ordnance Survey map which covers the Cheltenham and Cirencester area. In this poem she relishes the way the 'landlocked landscape ... lives in cipher' and how 'bigger than the hamlets they are / Wild wayside syllables stand blooming: / Filkins, Lechdale, Broughton Poggs' (ST:60; CP:102). The relationship between name and referent is notoriously complex and has been the subject of much recent critical study, but poets, from the Romantic period on, have been aware that names of familiar places hold within them and trigger on utterance the sum of associated memories. Wordsworth in 'Tintern Abbey' and Clare habitually (see especially 'Langley Woods' and 'Emmonsails Heath') are forerunners who particularly enjoyed playing on this complex layering of associative memory. The place names hold the sum of memory; evoke both recall and anticipation of the actual.

Fanthorpe shows how people are both encoders and decoders not only in relation to printed symbols, but in relation to each other. The tension between what remains constant and what changes, what is known and what is unknown in the people around us is always tantalising. 'The Other' is an unknown text. Fanthorpe remembers, in her poem '7301', the early days of her relationship with Rosie, 'Learning to read you, twenty years ago / Learning ... / How you encode teachers and classrooms / As *the hands, the shop floor* ' (AWB:33; CP:211-12). The title alludes to the fact that they have already enjoyed 'seventy-three hundred' days together, days which have confirmed the anticipated pleasure of 'Doing perfectly ordinary things together'. She feels she can 'Fairly reckon on seventy-three hundred more ... I hold them crammed in my arms, colossal crops / Of shining tomorrows that may never happen, / But may they!' The end of the poem acknowledges that the task of reading one's partner is never complete, 'Still learning to read you, / To hear what it is you're saying, to master the code' (CP:212).

The role of observer and recorder isn't a simple one. Just what is the significance of what is being seen / overheard? When Fanthorpe describes for example an incident involving a girl Koreen from 'The Remand Centre' she knows her cries of '*Get lost*' mean '*I love you*' as her blows caress her warder (SE:23; CP:29). How do we know the significance of what we are hearing and seeing, how do we know how our reporting will be construed? It is a problem felt particularly acutely in childhood, but it doesn't end there. Fanthorpe recalls in her poem 'Half-past Two' (NV:31; CP:262) an incident from her own childhood when she was trying to make sense of the language of time. (It is transposed here into third person masculine.) Because the child 'did Something Very Wrong / I forget what it was,' he is made to stay in the schoolroom till half past two:

> He knew a lot of time: he knew
> Gettinguptime, timeyouwereofftime,
> Timetogohomenow time, TVtime,
>
> Timeformykisstime (that was Grantime).
> All the important times he knew,
> But not half-past two.
>
> He knew the clockface, the little eyes

And two long legs for walking,
But he couldn't click its language,

So he waited, beyond onceupona,
Out of reach of all the timefors,
And he knew he'd escaped for ever

Into the smell of old chrysanthemums on Her desk
into the silent noise his hangnail made,
Into the air outside the window, into ever. (CP:262)

The run-on words cleverly remind us how much experience goes into sorting out where words begin and end.

Fanthorpe gives a wonderful insight into the problems of a small child trying to make sense of adult conversation about poetry, in 'Seminar: Felicity and Mr Frost' (VO:60; CP:169). This not only captures the atmosphere and dynamics of this session she was attending while in her residency at St Martin's College, Lancaster, but it also raises very fundamental concerns about language and communication. The tutor has had to bring along her daughter, 'Marigold-headed Felicity (three)'. Fanthorpe sees the child as one of the truth-tellers in the room, the other is the poet being studied, Robert Frost. The child who has been occupied with crayons none-theless struggles to make sense of the discussion and blurts out with a total lack of inhibition '*I didn't understand the story / The man was telling us*'; at which point the tutor confides to her students, 'Don't ever have children.' The comment seems all too meaningful to the child who repeats it back to the mother. '*You said / Don't have children*'. The mother tries to reassure: '*I didn't mean it*'. But the damage has been done; a spell broken, a secret world cancelled. Complex codes of tone and irony cannot be fathomed by the child who only operates on the literal plane.

Adults are constantly learning new codes and new forms of expression and are frequently faced with situations where they struggle to decode given signals. Most would recognise the context of the formulaic expression 'You will be hearing from us shortly' (ST:40; CP:92) which is the title of one of Fanthorpe's most popular monologues. In this poem an interviewee faces a barrage of questions. What looks at first sight like dialogue on the page, a pattern of question and response, is discovered, as soon as one tries to voice the poem, to be more subtle. The candidate's response to the panel's questions remains unvoiced or unheard. The pause after the questions, indicated by stepped caesura on the page, is in fact followed by the interviewer's voice again giving a minimal and discouraging retort to whatever answer was offered, implying through tone and register that the answer was unsatisfactory, not only in terms of fitness for this particular job, but for life itself:

> You feel adequate to the demands of this position?
> What qualities do you feel you
> Personally have to offer?
> > > Ah. (CP:92)

The candidate becomes increasingly demoralised:

> > Were
> You educated?   We mean of course
> *Where* were you educated?

> And how
> Much of a handicap is that to you,
> Would you say? (CP:93)

Without the job itself being specified, or the candidate given a name or gender, the archetypal dynamic of powerlessness is enacted.

> And you were born – ?
> > Yes. Pity. (CP:93)

Far too many are likely to recognise the demoralising scenario. The title phrase, though overtly non-committal, is often construed by candidates to imply their interview has been unsuccessful ... a formal letter of rejection will arrive in the post. (The Sophoclean echo at the end of the poem here calls to mind the bleak drama of this period of growing unemployment, Alan Bleasdale's *Boys from the Blackstuff* and his protagonist Yosser's catch phrase 'Gizza job'.) The poem bears witness to some of the typical struggles of ordinary people, the false assumptions made, the indignities suffered.

A patient watcher

Capturing such dramatic moments is also the task of the genre painter. Scattered throughout Fanthorpe's volumes are poems which take their inspiration from paintings, sketchbooks, or tapestries many of which encapsulate equally dramatic moments and reflect her fascination with the processes of visual artists.

Fanthorpe's poem 'The Doctor' (WB:10; CP:191) is a response to Sir Luke Fildes' painting which is reproduced on the cover of *A Watching Brief*. She directs our eye not only to the Doctor's absorbed attention to the child in the centre of the frame, for whom he can do no more, but also to the absorption of the painter with his subject. Her gaze has also taken in the concerns of the attendants, on duty in the Tate Gallery, whose troubled conversation about the ailments of contemporary old age frame her observations on this picture about the fragility of the Victorian child's life. Multiple framing devices like this appear frequently in her work affording interesting historical and social perspectives and allowing scope for ironies. She appreciates that the painters of this period 'knew about mortality', has recognised Turner's 'hectic skies', has seen the way Gainsborough 'eyed his lovely, delicate daughters', saw their 'consumptive colours' and 'gorgeous goitred throats'. Fanthorpe like Sir Luke Fildes and The Doctor is also a 'patient watcher' who has 'eyes for those who watch'. Fanthorpe attends to the fine details of the observed object or person or landscape and appreciates them all the more when they are under threat, or unnoticed by others.

This is the moment. I have trapped it.

Fanthorpe has a similar empathy with the painter Monet. Effects of light, changes in the weather, are a recurrent leitmotif in her work. She explains (in *Poetry Matters* 2) how her reading of a Gloucestershire farmer's diary for the years 1879-80 which recorded a period of 'disastrous harvests, resulting from an appreciable change in weather patterns' raised questions in her mind about who else was profoundly affected by the same weather. Research discovered connections with Disraeli whose asthma was aggravated by the London fogs, leading to his death in 1881, and to Monet. The idea became an obsession. She comments:

> I saw all three ... farmer ... painter, politician as people incessantly on the watch. The weather was centrally important to them, in quite different ways and was beyond their control (*Poetry Matters*, 1984:26).

Fanthorpe was awarded a travelling scholarship by the Society of Authors to enable her to pursue this interest. It was this sensational winter of 1879-80 following the death of his first wife, which provoked Monet into painting the notable series of pictures, particularly about the dramatic and destructive thaw, 'La Débâcle'. In *Impressionists in Winter* art critic Eliza Rathbone explains the situation:

> the rise in temperature that began on January 3rd 1880 after weeks below freezing wreaked havoc on the city and countryside around. The destruction to boats and trees was considerable as was the damage to riverside suburbs and roads as huge islands of ice floated uncontrollably down the river (in Moffett et al 1999:114).

Fanthorpe's poem 'La Débâcle: Temps Gris' which appears in the first cluster of poems subtitled 'Perspectives' in *A Watching Brief* (1987) begins with Monet specifying his viewpoint:

Seine Facing South. Midday.
No sun. Cloud heavy over Lavacourt,

No boat, no body. Water, Ice, Snow,
Houses, trees, hills, cloud sky ...

Not a thing here means
Anything but that it is here,
Now. I am the witness, bound to set down
What I see. This is what I see. (AWB:12; CP:193)

These last lines seem apt for both artist and poet. The following
stanza commands us to watch, purportedly with the artist, but
really with U.A. reconstructing his vision, his process, the way
'rashers of colour run along the slabsides' of the ice, the way 'water
and film and ice / Mirror the hummocky pink-grey cloud', helping
us see the painting in detail and understand the extraordinariness of
this moment when the ice melts, what it is about this grey scene
that captivated the attention of the artist, what it is that he has
caught. Standing back from his painting towards the end of the
poem Monet asserts, 'This is the moment. I have trapped it'
(CP:194).

Eliza Rathbone comments that this 1880 *Débâcle* series of
paintings show Monet 'exploring the quality of winter light on
water in an unprecedented way' in an attempt to 'capture a single
subject in all its moods' (Rathbone in Moffett et al 1999:114). This
concern with ways of looking, this sense of absorption with a loved
person or landscape in all its seasons and changes is Fanthorpe's
subject too. The two are brought together in 'For OS 759934:
14.2.96. A Love-poem', which is overtly a eulogy for her home
town Wotton-under-Edge, (discussed further in Chapter 4).

Fanthorpe recognises the same obsessions with light and
weather, the same painterly quality and finely observed detail in the
journal entries of Dorothy Wordsworth. Fanthorpe's poem 'Deer
in Gowbarrow Park', from the same section of *A Watching Brief*, is
a response to Dorothy's journal entry for the day (April 4 1802)
recording the walk by the lake which gave rise two years later to
Wordsworth's famous daffodil poem. William may have felt, as his
most famous opening line states, that he was 'wandering lonely as a

cloud' but he was in fact with his sister who had her own poet's eye on the scene recording the exceptional weather conditions, minutiae of the natural context that includes not only daffodils, but cows that 'cause a diversion / ... wood-sorrel ... / waves at different distances, and rain'. Dorothy is also aware of the social context, 'a sour landlady (*it is her way*)', the price of their lodgings, what they ate:

> ... all the random details, the furze bush
> Opposite Mr Clarkson's, dry clothes afterwards,
> William reading Congreve by the fire, how it rained
> When you went to bed, and *N.B. Deer*
> *In Gowbarrow Park like skeletons,*
> With, of course, *daffodils, about the breadth*
> *Of a country turnpike road.* (WB:14; CP:194-5)

All the italicised lines here are Dorothy's and Fanthorpe's poem draws attention to the quality of her writing, her ability, like Monet's, to show what she sees, to 'hand us that day'. It is a skill Fanthorpe shares with her predecessor.

Fanthorpe gazes in wonder at both the marvellous and the mundane. There seems to be a need in her poetry to record not just the exceptional world of, for example, the hospital, but also the extraordinariness of everyday experience, to say 'this is how it is here'. These words form the opening line of a poem celebrating the native bluebell in 'Conygre Wood'. The first stanza with its truncated sentence fragments suggests the notes an artist would pencil for herself in a sketchbook with detail of colour and texture; it also has a sense of a soundtrack attached:

> This is how it is here:
> Native halflight. Rain off the Atlantic.
> Rack of blue like sky growing
> A foot above ground. Hush. Birdcalls.
> Small puckered beech leaves, and earth,
> Its muscles showing, hurdling up limestone,
> With acres of blue on its back. (C:39; CP:374)

The unassuming native bluebell is classified as 'Hyakinthoides Non-Scriptus', which Fanthorpe reads as a 'snub':

> But our island gets this lot, illiterate
> Non-scriptus flowers. Growing along with garlic,
> Smelling of honey, careless of latin snubs.
> Blue and blue and blue and free
> Of an invented grief, free
> To come and go, to multiply, to chant
> The noiseless bluebell anthem: *here we are*. (CP:374)

The invented grief is the story of Endymion, the alternative name for the Spanish Bluebell. While the surface tone might sound derogatory about 'this lot, illiterate,' the poem in fact shows that what speaks to us is the amazing density and breadth of colour. The 'unmarked' native English bluebell has its own special eloquence. The voice given to it is that of the ordinary people, a football crowd, singing unpretentiously and emphatically 'here we are.'

Sometimes this need to observe and record is driven by the desire to communicate with an absent partner, as in 'Chaplaincy Fell Walk', where she records the idiosyncratic characters on the walk including, the 'one out in front / With superior calves and experienced boots'; but also the 'remote presence of hills / And the absence of you' (VO:66; CP:173). Similarly in 'Queueing Outside the Jeu de Paume In Light Rain' there is a clear sense of an addressee in this letter from abroad. (The queue would probably have been for the Monet exhibition in Paris.) The poem not only captures the texture of the day, but also imagines how it would have a totally different dynamic if the missing other were present:

> If you were here
> I'd ask the smiling African
> In my slow-motion French what makes his birds
> Rattle their paper wings, and fly, and fall
> Beside his hand. *Gilly-gilly-gilly*, he woos us all,
> *Very good, very nice*. For you he'd laugh,
> And tell. (AWB:36; CP:214)

Words are my element. Photograph them.

Fanthorpe likes to be the one, as in this poem above, doing the watching and reporting, not the subject of someone else's scrutiny. She is aware of being an 'Awkward Subject' in a poem prompted by the need to pose for a press photograph. She fears that the photograph would immortalise a false impression ... 'My casual adaptation to the place / (One hand in pocket, right knee slightly bent) / May not be what I mean, but is in danger / Of immortality /... Words are my element. / Photograph them' (NV:59; CP:283). But her eye often turns its scrutiny on the watching self and on the audience. One minute we seem to be invited to look in on someone else; the next we realise it is ourselves we are examining.

When she directs the photographer / reader to photograph the words, is the implication that the words will reveal the subject and / or that she will be invisible behind them? Does this relate to her use of masks and personas? She has said:

> I find it hard to get Me into a poem, so the voices of the other Mes tend to be the ones I prefer to use, especially as I can see their artful omissions, or self-deceptions, whereas I'm not too sure of my own. And because they're not me I can work at the unspoken things, the silence behind the words which is where I'd like the poetry to be going (from *Words at the End of their Tether*: 2-3).

Despite her intention to keep out of the frame of the earlier poems, an image of the observing poet is inevitably revealed in the process of drawing our attention to other subjects. She has a more definite presence in some of the love poems, and more recent poems of personal recollections of childhood. She lets us see at the end of 'Kinch and Lack', for example, her own childhood resolution to find a future for herself, 'O.K. I'll make my own' (CP:365), or her self realisation at the end of 'Mother Scrubbing the Floor' that 'I stand where she knelt' (CP:366). Both these lines are assertively singled out with a space before and after, leaving the self very exposed, with no mask in sight. Increasingly in recent volumes her own voice is heard; it may be a 'small personal voice', but it reflects the impact on the self of larger social and political issues.

There is a sense all along of Fanthorpe being in a state of readiness, but simultaneously watching the self that watches, as here in 'Confessio Amantis' a poem in which she adopts a series of personae including Dog and Dragon and also:

> Watchman, who waketh, generally without a clue
> Of what he waketh for; I am Spy,
> Watchman's other self, the double agent.
> (WB:41; CP:218)

The troubling sense here of a double, of 'watchman's other self' is a darker thread that can be traced throughout her work. She frequently captures in her images those disturbing moments when a subject gains a new insight or a disturbing reflection of themselves as other. In 'Seven Types of Shadow', there is a stanza that looks at those partial glimpses afforded by a mirror:

> The future eyes us sideways as we eye ourselves.
> We are the ghosts of great aunts and grand nephews.
> We are ghosts of what is dead and not yet born. (C:44; CP:378)

Silence has a better vocabulary

There is also the problem of those intuitions and understandings which can't be voiced. Traces of the past and communication between generations interest this poet. In 'The Silence' she remembers a moment in *The Aeneid* when the story of the fall of Troy is being told and within it an embedded story reported by Aeneas:

> A slave told me a yarn: some man, on his way
> From losing a kingdom to finding another, gave
> A friendly queen his story,

And her people stopped talking, and listened. *Conticuere omnes*
Something like that. Stuck in my mind somehow:
They all fell silent. (SAH:10; CP:292)

Clearly the incident has stuck in the mind of the poet from her
early lessons, as well as in the mind of the storyteller. Its resonance
resides in the double silence; the power of the original storyteller
which renders the crowd silent in an attentive listening, and the fact
that now both tellers and listeners are no more. They have all fallen
into the silence of death and only a few traces in terms of stories and
signs remain. Seeing 'Those curses they scratched widdershins on
lead – / asking for trouble' has a powerful effect on the imagination:

> Here we stand
> Between *Caes. Div. Aug,* and the next lot, expert only
> At unspeakable things,
>
> Stranded between history and history, vague in-between people.
> What we know will not be handed on.
> *Conticuere omnes.* (SAH:11; CP:293)

The final line seems ominously to look ahead to a point when the
writer of this version of the story and its readers will also have fallen
silent, almost as if the reading of the original brought home that
message about mortality.

As Fanthorpe says in 'Against Speech' commenting on the
Marx brothers:

> Harpo's the wittiest Marx. Words are only
> For what can be said; silence
> Has a better vocabulary (C:32; CP:367).

She enjoys adopting the personae of other watchers and, interestingly for one who initially felt silenced and muffled, these
personae give her tremendous power, authority and eloquence. She
is quite happy to assume, as discussed above, the voice of Christ, and
here in 'Gospel Truth' she opens in the voice of the gospeller John:

I am the one who sees
Whose eyes outshine the sun (C:53; CP:386).

The dramatic monologue is a device which deliberately alerts us to the distance between the voice of the persona and the poet constructing that voice. Yet in this poem, which gives a stanza and a voice to each of the four gospellers, it is hard not to see the points of connection between poet and persona. In many ways Fanthorpe is the one who sees, the one who tells. She could say, as Luke does, in his opening line, 'I learned my art in hospitals.' She appreciates this fellow writer Matt Simpson, the poet for whom this poem is written, as one who:

> ...knows the people's names,
> The shops, the cinemas, the docks,
> The pubs, the children's games;
> Who loves the living and the dead
> Of the place where he began,
> The holy city Liverpool.
> Matthew celebrates man. (C:53; CP:386)

Though Fanthorpe's place of origin and current home are in a very different area of England, it is clear that the qualities of attentiveness to people and places which she appreciates in this fellow poet are shared qualities. It was a painting of St Matthew by Caravaggio that prompted Margaret Atwood to comment:

> No wonder St Matthew looks so apprehensive ...clutching his pen while a thuggish angel dictates to him what he must write down: the act of writing comes weighted with a burden of anxieties. The written word is so much like evidence – like something that can be used against you later (Atwood, 2002:47-8).

This comes from 'The jekyll hand, the hyde hand, and the slippery double' a chapter of *Negotiating with the Dead: A Writer on Writing* in which Atwood explores the problematic relationship between any individual writer and the persona of author they construct when writing. It is prefaced with a quotation by Nadine Gordimer, 'The tension between standing apart and being fully involved: that is what makes a writer.' That tension can be clearly seen in Fanthorpe's work.

Fanthorpe's attempts at 'setting the record straight' take various forms. She can, as in 'Unauthorised Version' (CP:237-8) from which that line is taken, revisit stories that have been told from a partial viewpoint and see that there might be another truth there. Re-mythologising is a common strategy of the woman poet. She can do her best to make vivid and truthful moments of her own observed experience, whether it is of a bluebell wood, or an encounter and conversation with an outpatient. She can be true to her historic research and the personal experience of wars, the knowledge she digs for under the surface of the official histories. She can also look over the shoulder of visual artists and observe their attempts to be truthful to their observed experience. As here in 'Underground', a response to Henry Moore's *Shelter Notebook*, 'Round the corner the artist watches, / Jotting notes on an envelope'. He's drawing 'huge / Muffled forms, trussed and bandaged / Like Lazarus.'

> From their coding we can construe
> Houses falling, bridges falling. London falling,
> Civilisation falling down. The artist
>
> Must show this without saying. Just
> His sketchbook sotto-voce: *Abstractish figures shelter background,*
> And *Try white again then scumble dryish grey over.*
> (C:48; CP:381-2)

The italicised quotations are Moore's notes to himself about how to create on canvas the vivid impression of what he is seeing. What she also sees in these sketches are the seeds of future sculptures. 'Wood and stone / As well as bones and veins wait inside / These vast vulnerabilities.'

There is a clear sense that Fanthorpe too is 'the artist taking notes round the corner' (CP:383). The desire to record accurately as well as to set the record straight, about the self, about the past, about the present, is paramount. It is an attempt made in the full knowledge that:

> Truth is hard to translate
> When our only machinery is words. (C:62; CP:392)

One of the things Fanthorpe goes on to speak out about and witness against is war itself and its appalling waste of life, an issue which will be dealt with more fully in the next chapter. She herself was part of the 'Collateral Damage' of the Second World war and responds to the rhetorical question, 'Why write about all this now?':

> Because it took so long to disentangle the unconscious process. Since this has been a century of war and dispossession, many people in the future may find their mouths blocked as mine was. I'd like them to know they can retrieve and use their silence.

> So I write for the not-yet-poets of Iraq, Bosnia, Kosovo, Chechnya, Croatia, Rwanda, Palestine, Northern Ireland, Tibet; the places where war is or was, not over there, but here at home. You will have so much to write about, but it may need to be suppressed for years before you can deal with it justly. Don't worry. The great thing about poetry is that it will wait till you're ready. And when you are ready you will be summoned, as the great Russian poet Anna Akhmatova was. During the Stalinist terror, she was waiting in a line outside the Leningrad prison where her son was detained:

> A woman with blue lips standing behind me ... suddenly woke out of the benumbed condition in which we all found ourselves at that time and whispered in my ear

> – Can you put this into words?
> And I said
> I can

> We all have to be ready for the moment when that woman with the blue lips turns to us (WPC:210).

Chapter Three

Acts of retrieval and preservation:
England, its landscape, history and ways of life.

'This landscape is not given to forgetting.'

(U.A.F. C:10; CP:349)

Fanthorpe has had a lifelong interest in history. One of her major concerns has been from the start, 'the revision of history through the perspectives of the historically powerless or silenced' (Hacker, 1989:150). This interest expresses itself in her poetry in a variety of ways. Previous chapters have touched on her rewriting of myths. Several poems which will be discussed in this chapter illuminate the process of investigating the past through its traces in the present. Others show her as a keen chronicler of the present. Knowing how quickly 'now' becomes archived as history she creates in her poetry records of people and events embracing the nuances, rhythms and texture of ordinary lives that would be overlooked by the official historians. All sorts of closely observed detail of everyday lives creep unobtrusively into her work: details of language use, fashion, routines and habits, predominant concerns, social predicaments, which provide a record of history in the making.

She is particularly good at rituals and rites of passage and is adept at capturing the mindset and living patterns of characters from a variety of backgrounds ranging from 'Men on Allotments' (SE:55; CP:54), surveying their produce with almost spiritual reverence, to students with all their anxieties and uncertainties and potential selves suffering that first dislocation from home. She observes the moment when 'The First Years Arrive', an annual event for the institution, a special landmark event for the individuals involved: 'You could mistake it for a holiday / Rucksacks around, and Dormobiles' (VO:52; CP:163). (Clearly not this year's intake in their four-by-fours!) Fanthorpe knows it is a rite of passage not only for the student but for the parents; she catches both the public attempts to be bright and breezy and the worst private moment for the mother, back at home 'when she moves / An unneeded chair from the breakfast table.' In the companion poem, 'Being a Student' Fanthorpe empathises with the students for whom:

> the great
> Term revolves, like the gerbils'
> Wheel at home, and light falls
> In unique patterns each day

On the sea and the fell,
And none of it comes again ever,
So rich, so wild, so fast,
While inside me I haven't

Even arrived here yet. (CP:165)

Another annual ritual celebrated and preserved is the 'Horticultural Show'. In recording a lively wealth of impressions from this event Fanthorpe conveys a sense that it is a threatened species:

> Punch batters Judy, a man
> Creates a dry stone wall in thirty minutes,
>
> Arrows fly, coconuts fall, crocodiles
> And jubilee mugs disguised as children,
> Cope with candyfloss, the band
> Adds its slow waltz heart beat. (SE:58; CP:58)

Of the produce section where 'Sacrificed beetroots / Display their bleeding hearts' she comments 'we read the future in these entrails'.

I choose peace; I never get it

A rapidly receding world is also evoked through the voice of 'The Constant Tin Soldier' (ST:86; CP:120). This moving dramatic narrative recreates a very individual and idiosyncratic character and yet it also illuminates the type of damage done to thousands of unknown soldiers of the First World War who are counted amongst the survivors, but who, like him, may 'never recover from surviving'. She tells of the tic of terror:

> Picked up on a foggy March morning
> Between the Staffords and the Suffolks,
> Between Bullecourt and Croisilles.

You will carry this day like a tumour
In your head for life, fusilier,
And no one will ever needle it out. (CP:120)

Sixty years on and he still had detailed memories finely etched. In the first section of this long poem, called 'Breaking Day', the narrator structures the soldier's memories in a series of prompts: 'You remember the date: /... your place; /... the weather; /... the timing: /...' each of which introduces his account of the day that changed his life, that broke him; a day which 'rained noise / Mud, bone, hot lumps of jagged metal, / Gas, smoke, fear, darkness, dissolution' (CP:121). He remembers 'fear, fog, solitude'; his only choice, flight; the sense of being orphaned; how later after rehabilitation he still 'Yearned for the dead and the lost, / The officers, the other ranks, the men / I belonged with, who knew the same songs' (CP:123).

In the second section of the narrative called 'Spoils of Peace' he tells how:

On the frontier of failure I jobbed and prospered,
Natty, dapper, with my quickfire smile. (CP:125)

His use of the phrase 'shocking day' is just another cliché in the salesman's 'kerbside cheapjack patter' (CP:128). None meeting him would know how that first shocking day: '21st March 1918, Day / Of the Kaiserschlacht, day / Of the German Spring Offensive', a day for which 'the beaten have no name' (CP:120), a day which lives on with him and leaves a hollowness, reduces him to a tin soldier for the rest of his life, still constant, still standing to. The poem is a moving psychological study and though historically set it nonetheless raises questions as to how today's soldiers 'survive' the scenes they have lived through in Iraq or Afghanistan.

Fanthorpe is haunted by the historic and ongoing wastage of people's lives in wars. She knows all too well that, behind the apparently pastoral surface of rural England, traces of a violent past are everywhere reflected in its place names. 'Red Gutters/ And

Bloody Meadows are sprayed over counties' (CP:351). Her poem 'The Master of The Cast Shadow' contemplates the losses of the Wars of the Roses through the images of a painting:

> They don't see us, these sad mediaeval faces,
> With their crosses, their rings, their daggers, their painted eyes.
> They're on the watch for various ugly kinds
> Of early death.
> What they see is the weather,
> For the weather warred over England,
> As the roses slugged it out: fog at Barnet,
> Snow at Towton, three suns at Mortimer's Cross.
> (C:12; CP:351)

The statistics of mediaeval war appal her, 'They killed and killed and killed. Thirty thousand / In a morning.' She raises a far from silly question: 'Where did they find the people? / So few around, so many of them butchered.' This is from the title sequence of her millennium volume *Consequences*, seen by Kathleen Jamie as 'nothing short of a state of England address' (*PBS Bulletin* Summer 2000:15). In it Fanthorpe weaves back and forth between the mediaeval world and the contemporary. She began this sequence with a poem, 'Found on the Battlefield' when she arrived at the site of the Battle of Bosworth Field in Leicestershire on a narrow boat:

> Most of my beginnings have a geographical start; we got the boat and went up the Ashby canal, and it was getting dark; we didn't quite know where we were, so we moored up and in the morning... tremendous! The two standards: the Richard standard and the Henry, Lancastrian Standard; hefty things - not just little flags. What is all this? Where are we? – and it came from there really – we weren't intending to do all that (Conversation with ES, Wotton 2002).

Consequences suggests that nothing happens in isolation from the past or the future. A line isolated in the centre of the poem to give weight to its assertion proclaims in a typically punning way,

> This landscape is not given to forgetting. (CP: 349)

Fanthorpe, like T.S.Eliot whose presence can be felt behind this poem, knows 'There is no end but addition: the trailing consequence of further days and hours' (Eliot, *Four Quartets* 1959:37). Like him she is concerned with, 'timeless moments, the unattended / Moment, the moment in and out of time.' When particularities of the scene facing her are presented in vivid detail, they evoke a past. This can be a sociological past; the moorhen which 'slips into the water' in the opening line is seen as Neanderthal; but there is also a sense of a literary past; the observation that, 'Swans cruise, freighted with meaning' reminds the reader of their emblematic and mythic presence in poems such as Yeats' 'The Wild Swans At Coole'. (The problem of separating the real from the mythic is returned to in 'Another Swan Poem' CP: 394). Similarly the battlefield is both specific and of its type:

It is the usual battlefield, with a hill, a wood,
A marsh, phlegmatic cows, visitors' car park,
Disused railway, battle trails. And people,
No doubt with other things on their minds. (C:10; CP:349)

Fanthorpe imagines the heiress in her manor garden in 1485, wondering about the consequences of the outcome of the battle, 'Will it be King Dick or King Harry / That fathers my dynasty?' The poem moves from an anticipated future to the tawdry traces of a now distant past:

The precious things, the crowns and golden chains,
Are dirtied, and the fine steel basinets
Rot in the caked and scummy ditches.
Toilet paper standards flutter from the banks. (CP:349)

At the end of the poem the Queen's dilemma is reiterated and ironically placed next to a Hobson's choice of a dilemma over which contemporary planning battles are fought, 'will it be / King Dick or King Harry? Theme park or business centre?' The injunction 'Choose, England', with which this poem closes, is deeply ironic, given the lack of choice for most ordinary people about the context of their lives.

The second poem in the sequence, 'Lost and Lost' (C:11; CP:350) presents an equally barren view of the contemporary landscape:

> Richard the King is lost forever,
> Under the weight of Leicester City Centre.
> Above him trolleys, buggies, perform
>
> Their daily quickstep. Above him workmen
> Pitch and toss crates, mothers hurry and go
> With cars full of kids and plastic carrier bags.
>
> What mortal bones could resurrect from here? (CP:350)

The ironic injunction, 'Choose, England' (CP 356) is repeated at the beginning of the ninth poem in the sequence, 'Ask a Silly Question'. Fanthorpe, answering as she does in her small personal voice, so simple, so direct, so unequivocal, 'I choose peace', must be speaking for hundreds and thousands of her readers. Such a strong line in the poem; so impotent in real life. It is immediately rebutted:

> Takeovers and overtakers, de-militarised zones,
> Kings dead in ditches, displaced persons,
> Class war, sex war, civil war, war. Tortures,
> And other irregularities. (C:20; CP:356)

The present battlefield brings to mind others, 'In Rwanda, Lebanon, Bosnia, Ireland, here.' Fanthorpe understands that, 'with a nice feeling/ For euphemisms, you can get away with murder (CP: 357). The 'you' implicates the reader in some sort of acceptance of the 'anodyne lexicon' of such terms as 'Ethnic Cleansing' and 'Friendly Fire'.

One of the most haunting images, reiterated here and intensified from the opening poem of the sequence, observes 'Somewhere, all the time, / A dog is finding something beastly to eat / Under a hawthorn.' This together with the moorhen and the sea chewing away at the coast becomes a repeated leitmotif, creating an almost fugue-like effect in this sequence. Here it precedes a rhetorical question, 'Does it matter / Who it is, Harry or Dick?' A question that applies to the other litany of wars too. The image of the dog and its quarry persists disturbingly at the edge of the frame whilst Fanthorpe asserts that, 'What matters is that people live / The ordinary all-in-a-day's work life of peace'. From the global sweep of its vision the poem returns to Bosworth. 'This was the battlefield. Birds, hedges, sheep, / And long November shadows' (CP:357). As Eliot observed:

> while the light fails
> On a winter afternoon, in a secluded chapel
> History is now and England. (Eliot, 1959:58)

In another shift of temporal perspective Fanthorpe's poem homes in on the present and the parochial with a text also 'found on the battlefield' – a handwritten notice urging current parishioners to join in with '*Hedge laying / On Saturday*.' Totally unaware of its irony, the note reminds them in a rather patronising voice that this is '*a haven for wildlife ... Please do not pick or harm*'. In doing so it reminds the reader of what is at stake. The simple pleasure of enjoying the landscape is one of many that are cut short by war which ravages landscape along with its inhabitants. The final fragment of this collaged text is, as the footnotes explain, a quotation from a Punch cartoon. 'Who's 'im, Bill? / -A stranger. / 'Eave 'alf a brick at 'im.' This personal exchange is heard as coming from 'far off, the inveterate voice of battle.' And so the global and parochial are brought together; the connection made between local squabbles, intolerance of difference and full scale genocide.

We have no records of them

The basic questions raised in this sequence were prefigured in 'Unfinished Chronicle' the final poem of the 1987 collection, *A Watching Brief*. Its two main sections headed 1938 and 1939 document details of events for those years, interleaving the domestic perspective of the estate where the Sutton Hoo Treasure was discovered and exhumed with comments about the realisation of the approach and arrival of the Second World War:

> 1938
> A slack year on the estate, the men
> Hanging about idle. Mrs Pretty set them
> To dig the heathy tumps outside the garden.
>
> In this year the Germans marched
> Into Austria, and they held it.   (AWB:73; CP:241-2)

Following the historic find by the estate workers, Basil, who *'had a profound feeling / ... for the local soil'*, and Jack who *'was a green hand, / ... didn't rightly understand / the value of things'*, the archaeologists arrive:

> Clever lanky young men with pre-war haircuts;
> Eminent, emeritus now, with their pasts behind them,
> Retired, superseded, dead. (AWB 74; CP:242-3)

The speed with which news turns to history in these lines is chilling. When the gold, 'came out of the earth bright and shining / As the day it went in' what is described seems like a desecration and what happens to the treasure initially is seen as rather shabby:

> The winds of that year blew Redwald's flaked bones
> Over the fields of his kingdom. Gold leaf also
> Floated away in that weather. (AWB:74; CP:243)

The coming of war means the Treasure has to be 'stacked / In Aldwych underground for the duration' which raises the unspoken question, wouldn't it have been better left where it was? All this is, as Fanthorpe points out, 'long enough ago' but the final section of the chronicle brings us to the poet's present, a point at which the treasure is on full display:

> But high to this day
> In Londonchester looms the High King's regalia,
> Sword, sceptre, shield, helm, drinking horns and harp,
> Patched and polished, explained, made innocent, aimless.
>
> Behind glass, air-conditioned, they wait in their own way
> For what comes next. (CP:244)

The poem draws attention to the way these artefacts that are being revered and marvelled at are in fact far from innocent; they are the trappings of a war which, though distant, would have involved wasted and unrecorded lives. The looming of this regalia seems ominous.

So in bringing together and interleaving the unearthing of ancient history and the unfolding of the then present of 1938/9 and a war which could well have wasted the lives of Basil and Jack, Fanthorpe reminds us that history is continuous and contingent. She raises questions and concerns about the discrepancy between what is remembered and what is forgotten: the discrepancy between the power and narrative given to the leaders and the invisibility, the voicelessness of the ordinary people:

> Now Mrs Pretty is dead, who loyally gave
> The royal lot to the nation. Gardener Jack
> And brown-fingered Basil died too, no doubt;
> We have no records of them. (AWB:75; CP:243)

History hounds us

The way history is packaged and presented and how we relate to it, is a source of the poem 'Looking for Jorvik' (AWB:38; CP: 216). In this Fanthorpe syncopates her own observations with the small talk of the other tourists (yarns about how long they queued for Tutankhamen) and sound bites from the taped commentary in the Jorvik museum as they travel down this time capsule where 'History / Breathes them in'. They journey 'past *Pack up your troubles*, / Puffing Billies, factory acts ... The Black Death ... to the ancestral / Mutter and reek. This is then, now. We are / Where it was, it is'. She contrasts the banality of the activity packs which proclaim *Eric Bloodaxe Rules OK* with the powerfulness of the original story about 'the appalling/Icelander Egil' who had murdered Bloodaxe's son, then saved his own life through the brilliant Head-Ransom song he had composed during his overnight respite. It was unlawful at the time to kill in hours of darkness. The Jorvik experience also triggers a memory, unearths a moment in the poet's own past:

> Changing trains twenty years ago on York station at midnight
> Among kit-bagged soldiers, on my way to you,
> > > thinking suddenly:
>
> *I am on my way to life.'* (CP:217)

There is an interesting essay by Alan Clarke, 'Past Tense, History, Heritage and Ideology' exploring the ways in which the commodification of history via the heritage industry makes this shift towards 'experiential' representations of history through centres such as the Jorvik in York, which he sees as 'skilful and insidious ways of managing the present through representing the past' (in Knauer and Murray, 2000: 73). He sees them as offering 'a particular history which consists almost exclusively, of individual and national continuity, of settled and certain meanings which are intended to pacify, occupy and reorient us' and above all which don't ask the question *why*? Fanthorpe's poems do pose that question and offer a critique of the packaging of history, what as a nation we choose to remember, and what we choose to forget.

This is clear in 'Dying Fall' (SAH:28; CP:309) which is a response to that most English of traditions, Remembrance Sunday, where she's aware of the huge gap between, 'The washed dim names that no one remembers, / Who died in a muddle of bugle calls' and the 'fitful drumbeat of glory'. She balances the weight of 'the bully band' which is 'irresistible, dammit. I choose not to conform, / I don't want to fight, but by jingo, jingo, jingo ...' with the 'tongueless bells' of the skulls of the dead, 'miming their message, / Waiting for the wind to say' (CP:309). To say what? The sentence which returns us to the opening couplet of this poem is poignantly left incomplete and leaves perhaps more than the traditional two minutes of silence to reflect what that message would be.

The popular fascination with history and the need to know is explored in 'Queueing for the Sun in Walbrook' the title poem of her 2003 collection. Queueing itself is something that fascinates Fanthorpe, interested as she is in time. This standing time, the suspension from other activity in anticipation of something special, is often a fruitful time for Fanthorpe. It is used for close observation and reflection. A time for her to write. She opens the poem with the comment, 'The first great London queue' (Q:9; CP:415). It is another poem which presents a collage of registers. Fanthorpe interleaves the headlines from London's evening papers at the time of this archaeological dig (1954), 'CROWDS SEE EIGHTEEN-HUNDRED-YEAR-OLD / ROMAN GOD DUG UP' with the voices of politicians and civil servants, Latin inscriptions from the relics, and her own reflections on this unearthing and its significance.

She imagines the most startling thing about this head of Mithras that had first begun to come to light on one of the worst nights of the Blitz in 1941 would have been its 'far-seeing / Merciful eyes' (CP:415). Mithras is the God of light and sun amongst the Persians. 'On the day's last dig,' she envisages 'the god's head, /

Decapitated, dirty, alien, moving' (CP416). What they have queued to see is 'Something outlandish, risen from London earth'. Despite the irony of the temple being reinvented in Queen Victoria Street 'in the wrong place, not far enough down, / Looking the wrong way' she ends with the affirmation that 'the sun / Remains unconquered'.

Fanthorpe's awareness of the way that 'history hounds us' continues in this latest volume *Queueing for the Sun*. In her poem 'Driving South' (Q: 26; CP:431) she contrasts the uneventfulness of the journey in which 'sun, trees and cooling towers become a dream', with the awfulness of the brutal historic events signalled by the place names they pass. It is Towton that shocks them out of their sense of tranquillity, 'What's done is quivering here, alive and dying' and they pass the place where 'Hundreds of peasants slowly starved to death:

> The bloody names pursue. York, Selby, Richmond,
> Pomfret, where Richard died. History hounds us.
> The sign posts stretch like hands, bonefingered, endless,
> Pointing us to a sorrow we can't share,
> Scorning our ignorance, compelling knowledge (CP:431).

They sense 'enormous sufferings behind each hedge' and realise 'suffering riddles England' (CP:431). A stop for petrol brings them back to the present where the grim face of the attendant suggests unknown domestic grief and the overflowing rubbish bins prompt the comment, 'How can they hold the litter of the past?' There is a sense that enlightenment about the past is paradoxically a burden.

Hauntings / Palimpsests

What interests Fanthorpe especially is how the traces of the past which remain in the landscape can be read. She enjoys investigating the stories behind inscriptions, names, signs, relics. She is rigorous in pursuing the truth beneath the surface. She ends the first section of *Side Effects* with a self-titled 'Palimpsest'. The poem's structure reflects its content; a palimpsest is a manuscript from which one text has been erased to make room for another, but the traces of the first remain visible. The italicised lines here are read as a second stanza which describes the way light, at certain times of day, throws into relief signs of the former use of the land:

> Once the surface of the ground has been
> *The sidelong eyes of dawn and twilight*
> disturbed, the effect is, for all practical
> *catch in the net of their long shadows*
> purposes, permanent: the perfect
> *what is no longer there: the grass offers*
> vestigial of a temple, as
> *its mute sermon on earth's derangement;*
> easily discernible in the
> *invisible and indelible*
> corn as on paper
> *as children's hatred.* (SE:40; CP:44)

This insight into the way aspects of the past are revealed when we look closely at a scene in a particular light, draws together her interest in landscape, history and those qualities of light that inform an artist's eye. In addition, the final image of these italicised lines, '*indelible as children's hatred*' is almost shocking, introducing a new context into the poem and connecting the physical, geological process of the layering of history with the layering of experience and memory that leaves its mark on personal psyches.

This connection between geographic and psychological strata is made again, even more powerfully, in 'Rising Damp' (ST:16; CP:71) in which Fanthorpe reflects on the way the hidden 'under-ground' rivers of London (whose names, 'Effra, Graveney, Falcon, Quaggy / Wandle, Walbrook, Tyburn, Fleet' form a litany or chorus within the poem) still have ways of making their presence felt. Despite the fact the names are now 'disfigured, / frayed, eff-aced' she knows these rivers which 'lie low' tend to 'return spect-rally after heavy rain', or 'infiltrate / chronic bronchitis statistics'.

With a rhythm reminiscent of 'This was the House that Jack Built', she explores the historic significance of these rivers in shaping London:

> There are the currents that chiselled the city,
> That washed the clothes and turned the mills,
> Where children drank and salmon swam
> And wells were holy. (CP:71)

The final stanza makes a comparison between London's underground rivers and those rivers from Greek mythology, which have come to represent the underground currents of our human psyche, our deepest fears and desires, our awareness of our mortality.

Fanthorpe had worked on this poem over a period of four years, and it had lain dormant in notebooks for some time. Only after her mother's death did she realise what it was really about and it reached completion:

> It is the other rivers that lie
> Lower, that touch us only in dreams
> That never surface. We feel their tug
> As a dowser's rod bends to the source below
>
> *Phlegethon, Acheron , Lethe, Styx.* (CP: 72)

As with many of her best poems, 'Rising Damp' straddles many worlds. The title implies not only a threat to the bricks and mortar of our lives, but metaphorically to those things which can surface from memory and overwhelm us psychologically. Writers as far back as De Quincey have seen the human brain 'as a palimpsest, in which all the layers of our feelings and memories coexist' (in *Suspiria de Profundis* cited in Lee, 2005:95.) The poem alludes to information from geological discourse, to legends, to nursery rhyme, social history, mythology, psychology, and all these different threads are brought together in a way that is simultaneously lyrical, playful and profound.

In a much later sequence of poems called 'Seven Types of Shadow' she explores the ghosts of the past in landscape:

This is a country of ghosts. Down the eastern shore
Lie the drowned villages, drowned luggers, drowned sailors.

After a hot summer, fields grow talkative.
Wheat speaks in crop marks, grasses in parch marks.

Wheat or grass, what they tell is the truth
Of things that lay underneath five thousand years ago,

The forts, the barrows, the barns, the shrines, the walls.
These are the native ghosts. (C:44; CP:378)

What comes across is a sense of poignancy, a sense of loss. People's voices are absent. Their life and way of life is gone. The fields and the surviving relics of human activity are all that are left to tell a human story. The other unspoken story and question is that of the present surveyor of the scene and the reader ... what will remain of us and all that our life has been. What is being recorded is a sense of being part of an inexorable process.

The next poem in this sequence explores 'our human ghosts', the images that face us when we look in the mirror as we age; the image we see contains a genetic map of our ancestors. Fanthorpe's metaphorical use of the phrase 'contours' links the mapping of the body with the mapping of landscape; 'their contours came by way of a long retinue / Of dust. We are photofits of the past' (C:44; CP:378).

Her approach to this commission from the Royal Festival Hall – write a ghost poem lasting 13 minutes! – is very subversive. She realises the whole notion of ghosts is 'fossilised' ... 'something un-conventional's needed'; so in one of the lighter sections of this sequence she imagines the ghosts of happy rather than tragic moments:

Voices calling, *I've passed / We won /*QED
It didn't hurt much, Mum / *They've given me the job*
I have decided to name this apple Bramley. (CP:379).

And even here that spirit of political subversiveness erupts, as Fanthorpe imagines the ghosts of moments of resistance, 'the women convicts singing their Holloway march/ While Ethel Smyth conducts from her cell with a toothbrush' (CP:380) and there is a sense of defiant celebration with 'the singers, the dancers, the liberated/ Holding hands and cheering in parks, while the tanks/ Squat immobilised' (CP:380).

There is a complex pattern of hauntings in much of Fanthorpe's poetry. 'The Middle Passage' from The Bristol Triptych, invokes the 'sombre absent presences' of those 'whom Bristol never saw', who supplied the apparently innocent cargoes of 'sugar, rum, tobacco' on which Bristol's wealth was based; the slaves who were 'shipped like cattle' who were 'sold / On the Guinea coast for cloth, / Jet, beads, muskets, spirits, trinkets' (NV:48; CP:274). These ghostly presences have no voices.

Marginal lands

Once established as a poet and working away from home on residencies, Fanthorpe explores and responds to those landscapes of exile which often also evoke a history of exploitation. Sunderland Point, on the Lancashire coast for example, is an inhospitable place, 'where sea, wind, sky / Dispute dominion, on a spur of land / so bitter that you'd think no one would take the trouble to go there' (WB:54; CP:228). Here she finds the burial place, in, 'of course, unconsecrated ground' of SAMBO:

A faithful NEGRO, who (attending his Master
From the West Indies) DIED
On his Arrival at Sunderland.

At first she comments:

> Sam lies very low.
> You can allow him any voice you like.
> Despair, pneumonia, exile, love, are variously
> Thought to have killed him. (CP:228)

Addressing his spirit she realises: 'You, who so clearly were not /
Your own man, lying in no man's land, /... seem in your muteness /
To be meaning something' (CP:229). This is one of the many
poems in which she shows her awareness in the background of the
inexorable erosion of land by water, 'The Ribble bites its banks, and
the sea gnaws at the shore' (CP:229).

This seems to have its counterpart in the erosion of values and
ways of life, a concern which increases as her work progresses. In
'A Major Road for Romney Marsh' Fanthorpe celebrates this
marginal land:

> It is a kingdom, a continent.
> Nowhere is like it.
>> (Ripe for development)
>
> It is salt, solitude, strangeness.
> It is ditches, and windcurled sheep.
> It is sky over sky after sky.
>> (It wants hard shoulders, Happy Eaters,
>> Heavy breathing of HGVs)
>
> It is obstinate hermit trees.
> It is small truculent churches
> Huddling under gale force.
>> (It wants WCs, Kwiksaves,
>> Artics, Ind Ests, Jnctns)
>
> It is the Military canal
> Minding its peaceable business,
> Between the levels and the Marsh.
>> (It wants *investing in roads*,
>> Sgns syng T'DEN, F'STONE, C'BURY)

It is itself, and different.
(Nt fr lng. Nt fr lng.)
(SAH:315; CP:315)

Speculating eyes view this unique and marginal land as 'ripe for development' and Fanthorpe interleaves these stanzas listing the virtues of the place with an offset litany of what developers see as its apparent 'wants' creating a counterpoint which voices a sense of threat. '(It wants WC's, Kwiksaves / Artics, Ind Ests, Junctions)'. The ugly truncated language of roadsigns shows Fanthorpe's despair at the obvious potential diminishment of a very special place whose intrinsic merits count for nothing with the developers. To voice the final line, 'Nt fr lng, Nt fr lng' involves the reader in a restorative act of reinserting the missing vowels.

She is particularly sensitive to homelessness and the threat to people's homes. In 'Counting Song' which plays with the nursery refrain of 'one man and his dog' she observes in London what has become an all too familiar sight, one of the 'waste people, grazing in litterbins, / Sleeping in cardboard, swaddled in broadsheets / And Waitrose plastic bags' with the inevitable dog:

> Not always the same dog,
> But the man looks the same, disposable,
> Scrapped. Hungerford Bridge his meadow. (SAH:31; CP:312)

She shows a similar compassion in 'Widening the Westway' (C:50; CP:383) for those evicted from the 'avenue-full of confident thirties semis' along this approach to London which is the target of the developers. The houses themselves are seen as sentient. The opening lines draw comparisons with images of the destruction of homes in other cultural contexts:

> Torched, they might have been, in another country
> Because the wrong people lived in them. (CP:383)

They are 'groomed for a protracted ending.' The stages in the process are revealed, how the experts, 'blinded each window ... extracted knockers and bells like teeth,' how they await the finishing blow when 'JCB's will rubbish the garlanded plaster.' All this under the appalled eyes of the houses opposite 'watching speechless'. 'Atrocity', she concludes, 'Is what we haven't got used to yet' (CP:384). The helplessness of people in the face of bureaucratic systems moves her, and the acts of vandalism of planning authorities are deemed to be not that far removed from the more obviously shocking scenes witnessed at a distance. This particular battle will be too trivial to appear even as a footnote in the history books but it is one that she has thought sufficiently important to record.

In a birthday poem for Prince Charles, 'A Brief Resumé at Fifty' (Q:60; CP:449), she reminds the Prince that 'this fragile special island, mauled by the sea', is 'Frittered away by speculators, eaten / By money-grubbers' (CP:450). Fanthorpe finds contemporary resonances in a comment of Burke's from *Reflections on the Revolution in France*: 'The age of chivalry is gone. That of sophisters, economists and calculators has succeeded.' She places this as an epigraph to 'Ask as Silly Question'; it could equally well have prefaced that earlier poem 'Not My Best Side' which showed the distance between the chivalry associated with England's patron Saint and the realities of life in contemporary Britain.

Her cynicism about this reductive process of commodification comes to fruition in *Consequences* with 'Autumn Offer' (C: 72; CP: 398) which shows the depth of her despair about the erosion of the liberal arts in the academic syllabus. She hates a world which wants to reduce everything to a common denominator. In this highly satirical poem the romantic lyricism of Keats' *Ode to Autumn* is reduced to the slogans of the material and utilitarian late twentieth century. The Autumn Offer comes in the voice of a marketing officer at a higher education institution, one of hundreds, which offers a 'leaner, fitter curriculum', where 'Already / we have axed from our course the modules that clearly / Have long passed their sell-by date: / Art, music, history, literature, religion. / Currently we are phasing out language, / But retaining Japanese and German, / For obvious reasons' (CP: 398). It sounds an extreme caricature of what was happening, but at the time I read this my own institution was in the process of 'talking economies of scale staff-wise', closing down the French department, decimating Literature Studies, closing down Art on our campus, and investing what scarce resources it had into more vocational subjects such as Sports Science. No longer a season of mists, but *'(Season of time-tables, and uniform ... Season of texts and learning what to think ... Season of learning to be like the rest)* ' (CP:398).

What Fanthorpe perceives is a society whose discourse indicates that it expects its youngsters 'to grow up/ Aggressive, acquisitive, mean'. In other words it reflects Thatcher's infamous assertion that 'there is no such thing as society'. The poem begins with the insight that what we are producing for the new millennium are 'consumers, investors and personnel'. It ends with the bleak throwaway remark that 'Most of life's problems can be solved / By running fast and kicking something' (CP:399). Fanthorpe's sharpest satire is reserved for those who disregard the human dimension of our lives.

Earthed

The need to look after England, the sense that 'it wouldn't survive automatically' is part of the legacy of her wartime childhood. The sense of anxiety is matched with a sense of enchantment, voiced here in a much earlier poem 'Earthed', with an allusion to *The Tempest*: 'This narrow island charged with echoes / And whispers snares me' (SE:26; CP:32). Later, in 'Ask A Silly Question' she shows her awareness of the limitations of an island in terms both of geographic erosions and insularity of outlook:

> This is all there is
> No Andes. No Outback. There's no more than this,
> And the sea chews away at Suffolk. (CP:357)

Fanthorpe's own roots were in the landscape of her childhood where she felt 'earthed ... in the chalky / Kent mud' and in the 'thin sharp ridges between wheel tracks, in / Surrey's wild gravel', but she also seems earthed in the landscape of Gloucestershire where she has lived for most of her working life. She loves the:

> ... serious Cotswold uplands, where
> Limestone confines the verges like yellow teeth,
> And trees look sideways. (SE:26; CP:31)

The relationship between people and the landscape they inhabit has always been important to her. Her home in the Cotswolds is app-ropriately slightly off the beaten track in Wotton-under-Edge. It's important for her to return from the 'exile' of residencies and home-in on 'one particular/ parish, one street, one house, one you' (CP:220). Her cosy apricot cottage contains not only book-lined walls, but also a reminder, in the form of a huge and brutal scythe displayed over an archway, of the far from cosy side of rural life in Gloucestershire. It is a testimony to the sheer physical effort that goes into the workaday world of the maintenance of the land. She is aware of the hands that have held it. In her poem 'Wotton Walks' (Q :52; CP:444) the paths around Wotton are valued not merely for present pleasures but the knowledge of the centuries of feet that have trod them: workers, fishermen, ladies, gamekeepers, gipsies.

Similarly, place names are savoured not simply for their taste on the tongue, their musicality, but for the history, the stories they inscribe and the experiences they recall. She has said, 'if a landscape appears in my poetry, it's because people have made it or done something to it' (Pitt, 1994:14). Even in a poem such as 'The Burren' (C 42; CP:376) inspired by a visit to this strange and unfamiliar landscape on the west coast of Ireland which begins with the comment 'Undomesticated', she finds a human story. What astonishes her about this 'great grey / Migrainous cramp of rock, / Squeezed, compressed and scoured / To treeless dryness' is that out of these apparently 'barren flags, this crazed landscape':

Jut the resilient heads of a melting pot
Of flowers from the high and cold, the low and hot,
The wet, wet places.   All at ease on this rockface.   (CP:376)

The resilience of these plants to the huge upheavals that created the
landscape seems to act as an objective correlative for the tenacity of
certain human beings in the face of all kinds of threats.

Incongruity and chance are important here and at the heart of
the poem is the point where geological accident and human accident
meet:

The boy out shooting rabbits puts his fingers
In a rocky crack, touched by the smoothness
Of a king's gold breastplate left behind
At Glenisheen.   These flybynight findings
Wait within gunshot in unpromising places –
Gold breastplates, gentians, happiness-ever-after. (CP:376)

The past's long pulse

Fanthorpe is always interested in the roots and history of the places
she finds herself in, even as here on holiday.   Many of her poems
encourage the reader to share that interest.   In 'Stanton Drew' a
poem from her earliest volume about a stone circle in the Mendips
nearer home, the reader is encouraged to see this stone circle afresh,
to strip away layers of subsequent history and think about the
original power of these stones and how, 'Still in season they will /
Hold the winter sun poised / Over Maes Knoll's white cheek, /
Chain the moon's footsteps to / The pattern of their dance'.   The
reader is invited to:

Stand inside the circle.   Put
Your hand on stone.   Listen
To the past's long pulse (SE:28; CP:32).

That long pulse is heard in many other contexts. 'Canal 1977', for example, another poem arising from a local landmark, demonstrates interesting shifts in temporal perspectives. Fanthorpe imaginatively reconstructs scenes both 'before' the canal was built and the 'not-yet after'. It is a response to a visit to the Sapperton Tunnel, which is acknowledged, because of its length, as the most impressive achievement in the construction of the canal and also the most difficult and expensive. Fanthorpe is aware of 'the picturesque antiquity / That savaged so many who made it.' Her poem draws on the contrast between the apparent peacefulness of the place and its appalling history that cost the lives of many of the Welsh navvies who built it:

> I remember this place: the conspiratorial
> Presence of trees, the leaves' design
> On uncommitted water, the pocky stonework
> Ruining mildly in mottled silence,
> The gutted pub, the dropping sounds
> Inside the tunnel, I remember this place.
> ...
>
>   Humanity goes out
> Like a light, like the Roman-Candle miners,
> Shafting their pits on a donkey winch, astraddle
> A powderkeg, light in their teeth, a fuse in each pocket,
> Lying foreign and broken in Gloucestershire churchyards now.
> (SE:57; CP:56)

Perhaps the poem began with the discovery of those gravestones and her empathy with those exiled even in death. Her early experience of evacuation give her empathy for exiles, whether the cause be work or war or even imprisonment, as in her poem 'Princetown' (ST:61; CP:103). Crossing Dartmoor and looking at Princetown prison she invites the reader to 'walk / The ripped up railway, its stonework/ The patient, perfect carving of cheap labour' and imagine the 'routine hopelessness' of the people who built this landscape. She contrasts the way the prison has been reduced to a tasteless joke on souvenir mugs, with the real heartache of separation glimpsed in the mother and daughter, 'arm in arm and crying / Outside the café offering cream teas.'

Many local landmarks have stories attached. The Tyndale monument can be seen from the road that climbs out of Wotton. It's highly likely that William Tyndale attended Grammar School at Wotton before going to Magdalen College, Oxford. 'Tyndale in Darkness', the sequence which opens *Safe as Houses*, celebrates the work of this translator of the Bible into the vernacular, 'plain English / All clinched and Bristol fashion' (CP:296) ... 'not the King's; / The people's; England's English' (CP:301). Fanthorpe empathises with his vocation and struggle, by adopting his voice in a series of dramatic monologues. She imagines Tyndale remembering a day when he stood on Nibley Knoll where his statue now stands, on the hill above her own home, looking out 'over moody Severn across the Forest / To the strangeness of Wales, Malvern's blue bony hills, / And down on the dear preoccupied people', seeing that 'the souls on the road, the souls on the river, / were the ones Jesus loved.' He understands his vocation was to give to the likes of the ploughboy:

> God's word,
> ... in his own workaday words. And I did,
> But it got so difficult: exile, hardship, shipwreck,
> Spies everywhere. Then prison, and the fire. (CP:300)

What inspires the poet here is not only the heroics of that tenacity of purpose in the face of such difficulties, but also the understanding of the significance of the task in terms of the changing power dynamics of the nation. It's hard for us to understand now what a lowly status English had at that time. Brian Moynahan, in his biography, *William Tyndale: If God Spare my Life* (2003), explains there were then only three million English speakers and even undergraduates were forbidden to speak English in the college precincts except on feast days and holidays. 'The English themselves largely governed, educated and prayed in Latin' (Moynahan, 2003:8). Up until then the law was with the Church, its rule not open to the scrutiny of ordinary people but only manipulated by an elite of Latin scholars. The powerlessness of the ordinary people in the face of this closed book and the revolutionary nature of this translation is what comes across in Fanthorpe's sequence. It conveys both the enormity of the project, and its potential impact. Tyndale went back to the original Hebrew for his translation; he favoured Anglo-Saxon rather than Latinate words. As Melvyn Bragg points out:

> Tyndale was not only bringing the word of God to the people, he was also, within that process, bringing in words which carried ideas, described feelings, gave voice to emotions, expanded the way in which we could describe how we lived. Words which tell us about the inner nature of our condition (Bragg, 2003: 110).

Fanthorpe's poem shows a double significance in his opening lines of Genesis, 'Let there be light'. This translation gave power to the people, illuminated their darkness. At the other end of the scale the poem acknowledges the importance of attention to detail; the need to find 'the human small-scale words / For the unimagined things' (CP:302). Fanthorpe, a translator herself in other aspects of her life, is imaginatively engaged with this task,

> *Sicut fumus dies mei*, my days are consumed –
> Consumed? An empty word. Eaten is better. (CP:298)

It is easy to see how this heroic life of Tyndale, with his passion for the English language and the ordinary people and social justice, undeterred from his vocation despite being denounced by Sir Thomas More as a heretic in 1523, hounded into exile and later betrayed, imprisoned and burned, inspires Fanthorpe's writing. Much of his translation was preserved in the King James Bible which in turn had a huge impact on the development of English:

> its words and rhythms sank deep shafts into the minds of the men and women who heard it. It went to the heart of the way we spoke, the

way we described the world and ourselves. Its English bound the English together (Bragg, 2003: 113).

In an interview for *The Poetry Archive* in 2005, Fanthorpe was asked how being English affected her poetry; in reply she talked of the sense of 'the specialness of England and the English language' which resulted from her experiences of the attacks on her hometown in the second world war. She adds:

> I was lucky that my course at Oxford included Old English, which gave me a sense of continuity because the language hasn't changed all that much, though a lot has been added. There's a pleasure as a writer in using such an experienced language, a language with so many words in it that you can use in so many different ways.

In 'Tyndale in Darkness' she imagines the particularities of Tyndale's confinement, what it would be like to continue translating 'with Death/ leaning over [his] shoulder . . . / Breathing at each sentence end' (CP:298). She contemplates what it would have been like doing this task in the cold and dark; and poignantly re-iterates the longing expressed in what we now know to be his final letter, 'for a whole shirt, and a lamp at night'.

The patterning of dark and light here and the awareness of totally different values of time, 'We have to hustle God / Who in His unhorizoned sphere of time, / Can hardly know how short our seasons are' (CP:302), resonate throughout Fanthorpe's work. The poem sequence creates a sense of Tyndale's thought processes, the attitudes and voice of someone himself a watcher and seer, someone committed to revealing through his translation 'the accurate voice of God' (CP: 302). His first translation of Genesis, in fact the whole of the Pentateuch, was lost at sea. So he started again. 'Twice I translated Genesis. I know / The deep places in it.' Fanthorpe's *Collected Poems* reveal not only the wit and humour for which she is best known, but poems like this showing her own knowledge of the deep places, the points of tension between faith and doubt, despair and celebration.

Chapter Four

Acts of doubt, faith, celebration:
the dark and the light

We each inherit our shadow, our ration of darkness,
That shrivels and spreads as light walks here and there.

(U.A.F. C:12; CP:351)

Neck-Verse (1992) has been described by Carol Ann Duffy as a collection 'conscious of staving off darkness and terror with the light cast by language'. In the same review Duffy comments that although 'bleak notes are struck ... which give the collection a coherence, a philosophy almost ... love saves; so do words' (Duffy *The Guardian* 02/07/92: 26). This chapter will explore the tension between the light and the dark throughout Fanthorpe's work.

One of the shadows or darknesses Fanthorpe has had to contend with for many years is the recurrence of clinical depression. In her essay 'Walking in Darkness' published in the psychiatric journal *Open Mind* she talks about the problems of the invisibility of this illness; how much easier it would be for those affected to have 'evidence of something wrong: a broken leg, a bandage, even a cough. Without such honourable scars there is a sense of shame, a desire not to tell friends, to keep indoors' (*Open Mind Issue 83*, 1997:20). It is something that she has never fully understood. She describes it as a predatory beast which 'comes prowling out of the darkness, itself a thing of darkness that disables for a time. Then, unpredictably but mercifully, it crawls off my back and goes away' (ibid).

This image of a beast is not dissimilar to those used by other sufferers: Churchill for example referred to his depression as "Black Dog". As Anthony Storr explains in his book *Churchill's Black Dog*, the fact that he had this nickname for depression suggests 'it was all too familiar a companion' (Storr, 1990:5). The philosopher and critic Julia Kristeva likens the descent of depression to a black sun and asks 'Out of what eerie galaxy do its invisible, lethargic rays reach me, pinning me down to the ground, to my bed, compelling me to silence, to renunciation?' (Kristeva,1989:3). Fanthorpe confides in her essay how the poem 'Inside' published in *Standing To* (1982) was in fact about herself and her experience of this condition and how 'with low cunning' she 'hid it among poems of the illnesses of other people' (*Open Mind* 1997:21).

This poem begins in an almost matter-of-fact tone explaining the existence of the parallel world of depression by analogy with a physical illness which can be revealed by x-ray:

> Inside our coloured, brisk world,
> Like a bone inside a leg, lies
> The world of the negative. (ST:28; CP:80)

Vivid and disturbing images then do their own x-ray work leading us into a terrifyingly surreal world of 'hypnotic clocks and unfinished / Goblin gestures':

> It is the same world, only somehow
> Conviction has dribbled out of it,
> Like stuffing from a toy. (CP:80)

She describes the sense of having 'lost touch with the sustaining / Ordinariness of things' and inhabiting a world where 'malevolence is routine, the shadow / Is real and the world is shadow.' There is a feeling of sheer panic when:

> Suddenly the immense and venerable
> Fallacies that prop the universe
> Fail, the colossal flickering fabric
> Which we must believe in so that it can be
> Goes out. (CP:80)

Can a fabric 'go out'? At first reading this might sound an awkward mixed metaphor, but it is surely designed to illustrate that confusion between the real and the shadow. The colossal flickering fabric appears as a printed or woven image of the night sky and stars, metaphorical lights which can no longer lead and aren't really there. Is this something akin to Larkin's 'vast moth-eaten musical brocade / created to pretend we never die' from his poem 'Aubade'? (Larkin, 1988:208)

  When Fanthorpe refers to 'our' brisk world in the opening stanza, the plural pronoun implies that it is the world to which she and the reader belong. By the final stanza it is clear she feels herself to be 'the alien' and the reader is helped to share that sense of disorientation when wandering:

Endless benighted streets where innocent households
Laugh behind blinds and believe in tomorrow
Like the milkbottles at the door. (CP:80-81)

There is a Freudian sense of the uncanny here: at the time of writing, 'milkbottles at the door' would have had connotations of the reliability of quotidian events – so much so that uncollected bottles would have signalled a problem, a fall, or even an unexpected death. Here the commonplace and comforting has been made strange. The use of 'blinds' suggest the speaker in this state of mind knows her own world view to be accurate, and believes those who are clinging to normality are simply shutting out the truth of things.

A similar blend of the domestic and the uncanny occurs in the poem 'Familiars' in *Neck-Verse* (NV:29; CP:260). The poem's title has a double edge: what is familiar is well known, but familiars are creatures from early English witchcraft stories, some of whom worked for their masters, had magical powers, while others could be dangerous and maleficent. There are two familiars in this poem. The one in the first stanza 'thinks it's a cat / comes at me widershins out of the dark / ... croons in my ear / of things done wrong,/ of things bound to go wrong,/ of the four last things. Seduced by its attentions / its intimacy ... / I submit to darkness' (CP:260).

There are disturbing contradictions here; cats are very dear to Fanthorpe and 'croons' suggests a lullaby, something soothing, but the words of the song are all about 'wrongs', as far from soothing as can be, as if the listener is being seduced into some sort of deathly oblivion. Again there are resonances here of Larkin; in his poem 'Wants' he admits 'Beneath it all, desire of oblivion runs' (Larkin, 1988:42). The second familiar in Fanthorpe's poem is another 'imaginary' creature which 'runs ahead / as dogs do /... would come at my call ... Almost I think it loves me, / would show me the way out' (CP:260). Again there are contradictory pulls here: the dog in running ahead and demanding attention seems to be encouraging an engagement with life, a sense of forward momentum, but that final phrase 'would show me a way out' is disturbingly ambiguous: a way out of a problem? Or a way out of life? Although the poet claims control and agency in the final line when she says 'I haven't yet decided / what colour it shall be', it seems to be a delusion as the creatures have, up to that point, seemed autonomous.

These familiar spirits are also said to be able to inspire artists and writers. Many writers including Julia Kristeva and Anthony Storr cited above have explored the connection between depression and the creative imagination. It has been much discussed since Stephen Fry's 2006 TV documentary *The Secret Life of The Manic Depressive*. Whereas Fry claimed that many victims of bipolar disorder preferred to endure the aching chasms of depression without therapy or drugs because of the creative high they experienced in the manic stage (cited in John Walsh, 'Beautiful Minds' in *The Independent on Sunday Review* 18/03/07:30), Fanthorpe's attitude is far different. She has accepted the need for medication and expressed a longing to be free of the problem. There is no doubt however that it colours her writing. There is an insightful essay by Hermione Lee in her collection *Body Parts: Essays on Life Writing* which looks at the connection between the writer, the body and illness. It begins with an exploration of Woolf's essay 'On being ill' and her emphasis on the creative and liberating effects of illness, but moves back to the Romantics and forward to the present 'burgeoning literature of pathography' (Lee, 2005:90).

Fanthorpe's poem 'Descent' from *Neck-Verse* illustrates the way she sees her depression as a genetic faultline:

> Some unremembered ancestor handed down to me
> The practice of walking in darkness.
>
> I didn't ask for it. I didn't want it . . .
>
>   . . . I don't like darkness,
> Its arbitrary swoops of stairs, its tunnel vaults,
> Black bristly air, its emptiness. (NV:20; CP:255)

Fanthorpe has said in her article *Slow Learner* 'my poems are mostly, in one way or another, an attempt to deal with an area of darkness in my mind. I'm not able to shed light on that darkness, but it seems important to try' (in *Poetry Matters 5*, 1987:35). In her poem 'Explorer' (a poem first printed in *Neck-Verse* but not included in *Collected Poems*) a female figure 'Chooses somewhere unexplored. / Goes without gear, walks alone / Into the white-out' (NV:28). This could be an expression of empathy with a real explorer but the figure could also be seen to stand metaphorically for her own journeys 'in the eye of despair' where the normal binary oppositions of dark and light are paradoxically confounded. She has said that when in the grip of depression the only sort of reading she can manage is about 'climbers in the Himalayas. I suppose their struggle with height and cold are a bearable parallel for my difficulties' (*Open Mind*, 1997:21). This comment could have some bearing on this poem. The lost disorientated figure here waits for 'The Authorities ... [to] tell her where she was, / what she did'. This contrasts strongly with the attitude expressed in the poem 'Descent', another of this cluster of dark poems in *Neck-Verse* where the speaker asserts:

> This is my black. I alone
> Am the authority, and I know no further
> Than I've got, if that be anywhere.
> I inherited no maps' (NV:20; CP:255).

In 'Doubles' from the same collection, Fanthorpe talks of the dark distorted mirror image that depression offers in terms of a train traveller seeing his own face in a lit window as a train enters a tunnel cut through rock;

> Inside the tunnel the traveller meets
> Self not the same in the shadow that mimics
> His place in the carriage. (NV:23; CP:257)

Fanthorpe goes on to think of the darkness of those who excavated the tunnel working from either end of the mountain and finally coming together from their different worlds meeting their 'double' and asking '*Is that you, brother*, ... / in a different language' (CP:257).

The cast shadow

Fanthorpe's account of depression sounds very like the following description of the cast shadow by art historian Michael Baxandall in his book *Shadows and Enlightenment*:

> The shaped and often grotesquely imitative mobility of a shadow, like some parasitical animal, can also be experienced as the uncanny (Baxandall, 1995:144).

He goes on to explain that the extended connotations of the word shadow or *Ombre* include:

> ghost; chimera; unreal appearance, diminished trace; secret pretext, concealment; the domination of a destructive presence; threat.

Fanthorpe is fascinated by the use of light and shadow in paintings and particularly intrigued by the changing conventions of the use of the cast shadow. The art historian E. H. Gombrich in his book *The Depiction of Cast Shadows in Western Art* talks about the difficulties of painters in recording the appearance of the shadow which is 'elusive ... fugitive and changeable'. He points out a central paradox:

> because we cannot touch them or grasp them ... ordinary parlance often resorts to the metaphor of shadows to describe anything unreal ... And yet there are situations where the appearance of a shadow testifies to the solidity of an object, for what casts a shadow must be real (Gombrich,1995:17).

The epigraph for this chapter, 'We each inherit our shadow, our ration of darkness / That shrivels and spreads as light walks here and there (C:12; CP: 351) comes from Fanthorpe's 'The Master of The Cast Shadow' from her 2000 'Consequences' sequence, a poem which begins with the observation that:

> Some painters leave shadow out. The Master hunts it
> From source of light to where the last
> Faint filigree fingertip falls,
> Unthinking as a sundial. (C: CP: 350)

That reference to the sundial, one of the earliest uses of the cast shadow to tell time, is significant in this poem which takes her back to the mediaeval battlefield through her responses to a painting by an artist of the period. Fanthorpe empathises with the sufferings of the soldiers whose lives have been claimed by The Wars of the Roses. Her own understandings of and sensitivity to the horrors of wars historic and present which trigger memories of her childhood discussed in the first chapter could be a further source of this 'darkness' which haunts her. She reflects, for example, how, when the Gulf War began in 1991:

> I was distressed more than I could account for, and found myself in the middle of a poem I couldn't remember starting, called 'Collateral Damage'. Then it all became clear. I had in a way been there. I was part of the damage (WPC:210).

As Kristeva succinctly points out:

> never has the power of destructive forces appeared as unquestionable and unavoidable as now, within and without society and the individual. The despoilation of nature, lives, property is accompanied by an upsurge ... of disorders whose diagnoses are being refined by psychiatry, – psychosis, depression, manic-depressive states, borderline states, false selves etc. (Kristeva, 1989:221-2)

There is a sense in which these darker poems give Fanthorpe's work a grounding, a solidity, very much a sense of the real. The notion of the cast shadow can usefully be seen in metaphoric terms for that darker part of the psyche from which these poems emanate.

Fanthorpe is aware we all live in the long cast shadow of the past of both personal and global history. But the cast shadow can also convey the ominous sense of the threat of the future. The reproduction of William Collins' 1833 painting 'Coming Events' is used by E.H. Gombrich to illustrate this point:

> This painting shows a country lad who has just opened a gate and touches his cap – to whom? To the horseman whose shadow we see in the foreground. We know what is approaching by its shadow (Gombrich, 1995:53).

The sense of simultaneously being aware of the shadow cast by past and future on our understanding of the present is made clear in Fanthorpe's poetry. This sense of dark foreboding is nowhere more chillingly evoked than in 'The Fortune-Teller's Funeral' (C:25; CP: 360), the penultimate poem in the 'Consequences' series. This poem, which Fanthorpe says surprised her, opens in the voice of Gypsy Rose Lee asserting: 'The seeing has been my life'. This Romany fortune-teller, whose real name was Urania Boswell, was a well-known and significant character whose funeral was reported in *The Kentish Times* (5.5.1933). Fanthorpe would only have been a very young child at the time but heard and later read about this spectacular event with black horse-drawn hearse and people coming from all over. In the poem Urania tells how she often has to 'muzzle' what she knows by speaking in riddles: 'How many young women will marry twice, / How many lads die young in sand or air' (CP:360). Urania has no qualms however about foreseeing her own death; knows the day and the weather in April 1933 and even plans her own send-off. She says 'Such things need to be thought about before' but there are others that don't bear to be foreseen. As Fanthorpe listens to the train along the Ashby line near the Battle of Bosworth and thinks of other less innocent carriages, so Urania hears *'the see-saw rattle / Of goods trains in the night'* and asks:

> Whose death is this? I will not see it.

What country's this? A world turned upside down.
I refuse the seeing. (CP:361)

She has premonitions but refuses to see *The Devouring*, the Romany
word for the Holocaust.

An abnormal response to the light

'Few functions of cast shadow are more vital than the possibility of
enhancing the impression of light' (Gombrich, 1995:42). When depression lifts Fanthorpe explains, 'I do seem to retain enough
awareness of the dark to have an abnormal response to the
light' (*Open Mind* 1997: 21). She draws on a memory from
childhood to illuminate this: she always had an acute dread of
visiting the dentist as a child, but on emerging from the surgery
things seemed for half an hour 'so wildly beautiful, strange,
echoing.' She goes on to comment:

> It isn't possible to live at that edge of sensation all the time, but quite
> often now I do. The dark makes colours brighter. And I think I see
> what people's faces are really saying, and listen more attentively ...
> They seem clearer. More remarkable than they were before the
> darkness (ibid).

That transition from dark to light is explored in a more literal
way in a poem 'Post-op' (C:70; CP: 397) which deals with effects of
a cataract operation. She opens with a combative statement: 'Artists
are wrong about light.' She expands:

> They strew it
> Tastefully across landscapes, let it focus
> Thoughtfully on a forehead or a cabbage,
> Self-consciously walk down a reach of water.

She repeats, 'Artists are wrong' before going on to explain the explosive violence of her own experience as light suddenly reaches her unfiltered:

> Light comes storming out of its corner
> Dealing dazzling uppercuts to the eyes.
> *See*, says Light, *It's like this and like this*,
> Injecting the whole national grid into one lens. (CP: 397-8)

The excitement and exuberance of the occasion of emerging from darkness is illuminated by the liveliest of images; light is personified, 'Grinning like a mouthful of American teeth; / Fizzing and raucous like the mixture / In Dr Jekyll's retort' (CP:398). Even at the height of celebration here, that simile reminds the reader of the potential eruption and disruptiveness of the double, the alter-ego Hyde.

Fanthorpe's poetry frequently acknowledges the dichotomy between an outward sense of propriety and an inner turmoil. She's aware of the fluidity and provisional nature of the boundaries that divide sanity and insanity, sickness and health. In the poem 'Patients' she asks, 'what can be done for us, / The un-diagnosed?' (VO:21; CP:143). This sentiment is echoed in 'A Cold Start' where she explains she found the world of the hospital divided between *them* and *us*, 'the mentally ill and the apparently mentally well' (Raitt, 1995:10). In her poem 'Spring Afternoon' (a poem discussed by Frieda Hughes in relation to Sylvia Townsend Warner's 'In April' in *The Times* 02/04/07:6) a figure looks down with other employees from 'dark office windows' from the hospital where she works to the brightness of the grounds of Stoke Park Mental Hospital next door where 'Depressives and obsessives/ Call gaily to us as they play croquet'. They hear sounds of 'wild in-mates' who 'Shout their improper comments from barred windows'. Their illness seems to free them to engage fully with the Spring while 'we' who are 'caged in normality', can only watch 'dumbly' and 'feel that something – Spring? Or our sanity? – has let us down' (ST:38; CP:88).

Homing In

It is in the introduction to a special collection of poems *Homing In: Selected Local Poems* published by the Cyder Press (2006) for The University of Gloucestershire to mark Fanthorpe's connection with the area and their acquisition of her archive material that Rosie Bailey comments:

> Some poets write best when they're on the edge of despair, some when they're solitary in libraries. Except perhaps for the initial explosion of the early hospital poems, ignited as they were by anger at the patients' helplessness, a rooted happiness has always been the most promising seed-bed for U.A.'s poems, even for the darkest and most searching.

U.A.'s own observations in her autobiographical prose pieces and her poems suggest more than just the hospital poems come from this darker side of the psyche. There is evidence of these bleaker concerns continuing well beyond the early hospital poems though interspersed with more celebratory material. The point Rosie is making is that these can only be written about when U.A. is well.

It is clear that a rooted sense of belonging to a loved place and being in a long-term loving partnership has militated against extremes of depression and enabled poetry to happen. Fanthorpe explains in 'A Cold Start' that her finding a voice in poetry co-incided and was contingent upon finding herself for the first time in a relationship that made sense of who she was. In hindsight she re-alises:

> It is clear to me I couldn't start [writing] until I knew who and where I was. There had to be a particular conjunction of 'home and place and the loved one all together' before the engine fired and the journey began (Raitt, 1995:10).

Many of Fanthorpe's poems rejoice in the light brought into her life by this partnership. An appreciation of Rosie's vital and extensive support is celebrated in the ironically titled 'A Minor Role' (Q:56; CP:446) The responsibilities of this role include:

Learning to conjugate all the genres of misery:
Tears, torpor, boredom, lassitude, yearnings
For a simpler illness, like a broken leg; ...

She has to '[make] sense / Of consultant's monologues ... contrive
meals for a hunger-striker ... check dosages; ... [pretend] all's well, /
Admit it's not'. But the ultimate responsibility recognised in the
poem's final line is 'to make you believe in life' (CP:447).

The brightness of this relationship, 'suddenly finding, the one
I'd spent my life looking for; the friend, the listener, the joker, the
finder, the other' (in Raitt, 1995:8) follows the misery of a childhood and young adulthood lived in what she refers to as The Age of
Concealment:

As far as I knew there were no lesbians in Gloucestershire: and if there
had been I'd have been terrified of them. There were no books, no
Helplines, nothing but silence (Raitt 1995:6).

It makes one wonder how much that sense of darkness and depression came from the feelings of being different and not being able
to articulate that difference as a young girl; feelings that probably
arrived with puberty; (she remembers 'being caught bloody-thighed,
a criminal / Guilty of puberty' CP:161), a time which coincided
with those other miseries of exile on the outbreak of war.

Given the high profile of gay pride marches today, it is hard to
imagine what growing up in the repressive age of the early to mid
twentieth century would have felt like for Fanthorpe who was born
in the year of the trial of Radclyffe Hall's *The Well Of Loneliness*.
The Editor of *The Sunday Express* who led the campaign to suppress
it referred to 'inverts' as 'lepers'. Fanthorpe knew of this book but
dare not read it in her adolescence, or young adulthood, 'for fear of
the uncongenial home truths it might contain' (Raitt, 1995:6).

There is an interesting overview of the changing cultural construction of homosexuality in Nicholas de Jongh's *Not in Front of
the Audience*. He charts the way the subject which had been 'un-
speakable' (even the word 'homosexuality' itself couldn't be uttered

on stage) prior to 1958 had by the 80's become 'discussable'; yet even at the time of writing in 1992 he says on stage and screen;

> the signs of homosexual affection and desire, still retain their capacity to shock and offend. Homosexuals and lesbians are still liable to be outcast from their own families. The theatre which since Ibsen has dealt with the crises of family relations, and of the heterodox as opposed to the orthodox still has significant sexual business to conduct ... to do with the task of demystifying homosexual love and enabling gay men and lesbians to be part of both the families into which they are born and the complementary sexual worlds into which they go (De Jongh, 1992:190).

It must have been hard for women like U.A. Fanthorpe with a deeply Christian outlook and a passionate commitment to England to know that homosexuality was regarded as a pathological condition; male homosexuality was seen as a national threat, as something treasonable. De Jongh considers the religious and cultural reasons for the stigmatisation of the homosexual who was demonised and categorised as monstrous and suggests:

> The Jungian theory of Shadow Projection offers an explanation of the psychic system by which we scapegoat. Jung diagnosed humanity's aggressive and cruel drives as the 'dark side or shadow of the psyche' The superego, that complex of coercive agents in the self, ensured that we would observe the controls of our culture and that these drives would usually be repressed in the unconscious (De Jongh, 1992:6).

Doubles

Fanthorpe's own sense of doubleness, of an official visible self and a darker inner self, is hinted at in many of her poems. 'Sightings' from her 2000 collection *Consequences* begins overtly with a reflection on the discovery of Neptune: 'It was there all the time, the dark planet / That no one saw' (C:64; CP:393). In the second stanza she describes a common enough scene of defamiliarisation:

turning round after climbing up the hill from home to find it vanished, though part of her knows 'The town's there all the time, under the mist'. The final stanza considers the strangeness of twins who 'pop up everywhere' in Shakespeare's plays. Here in the role of a stage character she muses, 'There's two of each of us ... / But undistinguishable. There's one from Ephesus / and one from Syracuse. The audience knows, / But we don't. That's the point; the strangeness / Of the other who is the same' (CP:393).

The sense of doubleness could come from a battle between self-pride and self-alienation. In the times she was living through there must have been a feeling of not being oneself, of being self and other. It is clear to see from her autobiographical writings what an expansive and emancipatory sense of possibilities came with the discovery of her partner, affectionately known as 'Leo':

> We tumbled into speech, we talked about everything, the miraculous ways we were alike, the even more miraculous ways we were different. We rejoiced at traffic lights, because we could look each other in the eyes at the red lights. We must have been very noticeable, but we didn't care. We sat behind lighted windows and talked ... I began to write, because for the first time life had some sort of shape. I wrote ballads about imprisonment, gaolers, liberators (Raitt,1995:7).

Her own writings, which do so much to demystify labels show a common humanity, show attitudes which run totally counter to the repressive ones cited by De Jongh above, scenes of sharing and loving and grieving and celebrating and writing, which are in their own small way revelatory and revolutionary.

Janus

It is perhaps this same undercurrent of awareness of 'the other who is the same' that leads her to adopt the persona of Janus, the two-headed god in *Standing-To*:

I am the future's overseer, the past's master.
See all, know all, speak not.
I am the two-faced god (ST:73; CP:112).

An image of a twelfth century carving of the two-headed god Janus
in Ferrara Cathedral was used to illustrate an essay by Hilary
Mantel about the writer and identity in which she discussed the
notion that:

> The creative imagination is a place of safety for the dead where they can
> show their faces and be recognised. We have to conjure the people of
> the past so they can lead us to our future. The god that artists must
> invoke is Janus, the double-faced god, the guardian of gates and doors
> (*Guardian Review*: 12/10/02:6).

Fanthorpe has frequently equated, albeit tongue in cheek, her
role as receptionist with other mythical guardians of gates and
doors; In her poem 'For Saint Peter' (SE:16; CP:25) she confides 'I
reckon that, like me, you deal with the outpatients.' In 'Cerberus'
from her sequence *Four Dogs* the analogy is with the three-headed
beast, who with an aparently innocent manner 'wagged his ears and
tail at visitors, / Admitted them all' but sinisterly 'saw to it / That
nobody ever got out' (ST:12; CP:68).

But Janus, the two-headed god represents, as Mantel suggests:

> the duty and privilege of the novelist to look both outward and inward,
> to the past and the future, to the particular and the universal, to the
> parish and the world.

This seems an equally valid comment for the stance Fanthorpe takes
in her poetry. In fact rhyme itself is seen as 'Janus-faced' by the
critic Gillian Beer:

> Rhyme is retrospective. It ... draws us back to what has gone before
> with a new thrill of connection. Thereafter it is Janus-faced, leading the
> eye and particularly the ear forward to seek the chime, but with a
> ballast of sonorities generated in the poem's past. Rhyme makes
> memory within the poem. It practises recollection. It may also bring

things back uncannily changed (*The Guardian Saturday Review* 13/01/07: 21).

This is demonstrated in Fanthorpe's poem 'Janus' with its linked assonances and consonances, shockingly bringing the wake and the wedding together in the internal near rhyme:

> From All Saints to All Souls I celebrate
> The *da capo* year. My emblems are albums,
> The bride's mother's orchid corsage, the dark cortège.
>
> I am archivist/ Of the last divorce and the first kiss. (CP: 111)

Human, of all things

Her poems also archive the very positive landmarks in her significant and enriching relationship with Rosie which was formalised in a civil partnership in 2006 after many shared years. American poet and critic Marilyn Hacker on first discovering Fanthorpe's poetry in 1989 remarks that,

> It is only specified, and understatedly in Fanthorpe's *A Watching Brief* that these two faithful companions ['At Averham'] are both women: a pronoun, a noun, a revelation that perhaps took more courage on the poet's part because it was not being made as a stance, or a political statement. Although it is one nevertheless. (Hacker, 1989:156-7)

'At Averham' revisits the scene of her father's early childhood, and reflects on the trajectories of their two fathers' lives:

> They might have met, two cherished children,
> Among nurses and buttercups, by the still silver Trent
>
> But didn't. That other implacable river, war,
> Trawled them both in its heady race. (AWB: 27; CP: 206)

She thinks of the issue of chance in encounters, 'two fathers who never met, / Two daughters who did' and comments 'You like the sound of my father. He would/ Have loved you plainly, for loving me.' The early phase of the daughters' lives together is revealed in Fanthorpe's 'Elegy for a Cat' from *Neck Verse* which shows the cat is mourned, not only for itself, but as 'the first to join our outlandish outfit / On that hilltop housing estate [in Merthyr Tydfil]:

First to live with us, first to confirm
Us as livers-together, you who took us so simply
For granted, translator of life into
The vernacular of love.
You who saw love, where innocent others
Saw only convenience. (NV:25; CP:259)

In poem '7301' (AWB:32; CP:212) thinking back seven thousand three hundred and one days to the early stages of her relationship she remembers 'learning to hide / The sudden shining naked looks of love' and projecting forward the excitement of a shared future 'doing perfectly ordinary things together – riding / In buses, walking in Sainsbury's, sitting / In pubs eating cheese and onion rolls.' These sorts of shared domestic routines any heterosexual couple would be able to take for granted seem to be especially celebrated.

She has said, 'apart from the love poems, and I only wrote them under extreme pressure from other people – I haven't written much about homosexuality (Raitt, 1995:10). A sensitivity to the public perception of it as a deviation from the norm is glimpsed in the poem 'Christmas Presents' which records a stay in hospital awaiting results of tests:

The local wise man had come up with gold:
A benign cluster. You'll be home by Christmas.

Nothing to say. When I was tired, we held hands.

But next bed's visitors were staring.

Why us? The colour of our hair. Perhaps? (SAH:65; CP:342)

On the following day when the neighbour's bed is stripped, she rethinks this and hypothesises an alternative reading: the woman's family had needed to avert their eyes from the sight of 'death creeping up and down her face';

> somewhere to rest their smarting eyes, but also
> (I like to think) because we were,
> Of all things, human;
>
> Human, of all things. (CP:343)

This poem places the emphasis firmly not on difference, but on common mortality and humanity.

Celebrations

This poem which first appeared in public in *Safe As Houses* is one of many poems gathered together in a special collection of *Christmas Poems* published by Peterloo Poets and Enitharmon Press in 2002. The first home-made card celebrating Christmas and its redemptive message was originally produced at home on their Culverhay Press for family and friends in 1972. This began a tradition that became a part of the pattern of Fanthorpe and Bailey's year, and testifies to the importance of faith in Fanthorpe's life.

There are several problems, as Fanthorpe and Bailey point out in their introduction, in keeping up with this tradition. First there is the wide age range of the initial audience of family and friends from toddlers to great-grandparents. Then there's the challenge of visiting anew a story with a limited cast list. They solved this by roping in absentees: 'the sheepdog left behind to look after the sheep (Ch:33) ... the cat who ought to have been there even if the evangelists failed to notice it' (Ch:45). There are also 'the idiosyncrasies of the printing process': the difficulties of the hand press, of founts, graphics, deadlines, line lengths. But the most touching insight in the introductory note is the way Fanthorpe and Bailey offer these poems on this most celebratory of themes in the hope that 'they may be useful, in the way of small, unpretending, domestic things' (Ch:8).

Christmas Poems are wittily illustrated by Nick Wadley; an image of a moon-like dial accompanies the poem 'BC:AD' which is featured on the cover. Bailey points out 'Quakers rightly maintain that Christmas Day is only one of three hundred and sixty five important days' (LP:8). Each of its stanzas focuses on and annotates the import of the moment of Christ's birth, a moment signified in the title by the colon between the two abbreviations, 'the moment when Before/ Turned into After'. As far as the history books are concerned it is 'the moment when nothing / Happened', history being a recorder only of wars. Each stanza becomes slightly weightier till the last sentence of the final tercet spills over into an additional couplet to complete the sonnet and express the enormity of that moment from a Christian viewpoint: 'this was the moment / When a few farm workers and three / Members of an obscure Persian sect / Walked haphazard by starlight straight / Into the kingdom of heaven' (CP:99).

In a more recent poem 'Not the Millennium' Fanthorpe comments on our contemporary wise men who 'are busy being computer-literate', whose scholarship casts doubt on the actual date and place of birth:

> The sources mention
> Massacres, prophecies, stars;
> They tell a good story but they don't agree.
>
> So we celebrate at the wrong midnight.

The important point, she insists, is 'There was a baby ... – Only dull science expects an accurate audit.' The poem ends with a typical Fanthorpian paradox: 'Be realistic, says heaven: / Expect a miracle' (Ch:61; CP:410).

The Christmas poems are witness to another tension in Fanthorpe's life, between a faith in the power of the Christmas story, and despair at the increasing commercialisation of this celebration in the late twentieth, early twenty-first century. In 'Party Night', a poem which first appeared in public in *Queueing For the Sun* (2003), Fanthorpe gives a calculating voice to a contemporary innkeeper, who turns away a couple:

> Saw at once they had to go –
> Not the party spirit.
> Him, living on handouts, no doubt ,
> Her, in the family way. *No,* I said to the wife,
> *Not this night, of all nights.*

He's resentful of his wife's obstinacy and act of kindness 'bedding them down in the shed'; while he's slaving away at a 'six-course corporate dinner' he missed:

> ...what the wife said she saw
> Fireworks, singing, comets, royals.
> Well, she may have. What I say is:
> Who made the genuine profit that night? (Q:92; CP:462)

'Christmas in envelopes' (Ch:57; CP401) interrogates the whole business of sending cards at Christmas: it begins in a cynical tone which seems to ask what is it all about? What is the relevance of the images on these cards, which have become part of the commercial exploitation of the festival, to the essence of Christmas?

> Monks are at it again, quaffing, carousing;
> And stage coaches, cantering straight out of Merrie England,
> In a flurry of whips and fetlocks, sacks and Santas.

The poem recognises a card like hers costs less in money than these but more in time; but the tone of the poem shifts and ends with the realisation that the essential message is 'Love' (Ch:57). And Love, along with Hope and Endurance is the essential Fanthorpe gospel.

The card sent to friends for Christmas 2007, entitled simply '2007' centres on the struggle between faith and doubt: its first three tercets open with the rhetorical question, *Where does the light come from?* The answers are far from complacent or comforting:

> Far away and cold the star
> And things are as they are.

The metaphor in the second stanza, 'Shepherd's lanterns flicker and go out / Like our faith, our doubt' seems to confer on doubt the same power as light. The poem ends on a note of acceptance:

> We wait and think.
>   At last we see
> Through Christmas, and that other tree,
> How things were meant to be.

It is clear elsewhere in her writing that she is very moved by narratives of those unwavering in their faith in the face of persecution: not only Tyndale, discussed in the previous chapter, but also Ralph Shirley, the unsung hero of her poem 'At Staunton Harold', who built the church there under Cromwell's rule and eventually paid for his disobedience with his life. The inscription over the Church door tells us that his praise is 'to have done the best things in ye worst times and to have hoped them in the most calamitous.' This poem which ends the 'Consequences' series rearranges those words so the sequence, dark as it is, ends on the note of hope (CP:362).

Several poems begin in holy places: 'Stanton Drew' (CP:32), the churchyard at 'Helpston' where John Clare is buried (CP:320), the ruins of Mount Grace Priory, for example, where she reflects on our imaginative access to the past and its people (CP:294). In 'Friend's Meeting House, Frenchay, Bristol' she thinks of the 'Rare herb of silence, through which the Word comes' and reflects on the work developed through such silent meditation:

In hopeless places, prisons, workhouses,
In countinghouses of respectable merchants,
In barracks, collieries, sweatshops, in hovels
Of driven and desperate men.

It begins here
In the ground of silence. (NV:47; CP:273)

Fanthorpe, as a Quaker, enjoys a faith which dispenses with a hierarchy of authority figures as mediators of worship and has instead a focus on private meditation. In order to come closer to God, thinking and reflection are what matter.

It is sharing the human condition and human connections that matters most, something that is celebrated in a range of contexts in Fanthorpe's poems. She rejoices in the camaraderie of writers in 'Workshop's End' a poem prefaced by an epigraph of Dr Johnson's: 'True happiness consists not in a multitude of friends, but in their worth and choice'.

We have explored
Bravely in difficult places. We've laughed a lot.
We've loved, not thinking much about it.
We've stayed together,
We thought forever. (Q:42; CP:437)

Elegies

Elegies are celebrations too: they bring together the dark and the light in recreating an image of the grieved-for subject. She writes 'Three Poems for Amy Cook (1909-1998)' a well-loved local figure who for years was a street sweeper at Wotton. The idiosyncrasies of Amy's mindset, speech patterns and dialect are embedded here:

At school they did teach we to remember.
When I did learn the alphabet, I did learn it
Frontards and backards. (And does it.) (C:36; CP:371)

Amy is a woman 'who endures, having learned over years to perform herself.' She 'knows how to tell her life / As if it were a story'. But the poet knows that she is much more than the part she plays of 'racy rustic', more than the statuesque 'pre-Cambrian hill' commemorated in the portrait. Fanthorpe remembers her 'Swift and surprising, like the road from Nibley'; and also 'her wit and her way with words' (CP:372).

These portraits of people, be they friends, neighbours or family are vivid and idiosyncratic, and none of them is sentimentalised. In remembering her friend Gwen, for example, she doesn't airbrush out the arguments, the 'worst coffee I've ever tried not to drink' the awful driving, the embarrassingly 'explicit obstetric stories'. She addresses this friend who had 'A knack of giving life', whose magnolia still 'sprouts fierce black buds' recreating her as the intended listener of the poem, giving her the congregation's perspective on the funeral service where they sing:

> *Jerusalem* tentatively, waiting for you to pop up and exclaim
> *You've left out the feeling.* So we have. I don't want to feel,
>
> Gwen, that you've ended anything. *I will not cease*, we drone.
> We haven't even started in the Great-heart way you did. (CP:452)

Fanthorpe ends the poem with the poignant rhetorical questions:

> What about Jerusalem? You haven't ceased, have you? (CP:453)

Similarly in her elegies for her mother and father she acknowledges the difficulties in relationships, the tensions as well as the underlying love and affection. In 'Fanfare', she sifts through photographs and remembers her mother's 'melancholy half-smile', recalls a woman who flourished in crisis, whose 'nightmare was Christmas: so much organised / Compulsory whoopee to be got through' (ST:10; CP:66). U.A. comments wryly:

> I know why you chose now to die. You foresaw

Us approaching the Delectable Mountains,
And didn't feel up to all the cheers and the mafficking. (CP:67)

She then asks tenderly of this re-embodied figure:

But how, dearest, will even you retain your
Special brand of hard-bitten stoicism
Among the halleluyas of the triumphant dead? (CP:67)

This was from the 1982 volume *Standing-To* published four years after her mother's death. She returns to capture other moments and aspects of her life and their relationship in 'Washing Up' in *A Watching Brief* (1987). Here she records her mother as a 'hater of parties' who comes into her own after the guests have left, doing her makeshift parodies of grand opera:

Deep in the quiet grave she'd serenade
The carving knife, from that a short step
To saucepans and the Jewel song: *Marguerita, this is not I.*
High born maiden I must be, high born maiden . . .
Her mezzo skidding along coloratura country
My laughter rattling the stacks. (WB:30; CP:209)

This 'doughty' woman who seldom laughed at jokes is also a 'sorcerer-mother' and 'magical' (CP:210), a much more sparkling memory here in this virtuoso piece, than 'Mother Scrubbing the Floor'.   In this she records her mother quoting a disconsolate statement from Shaw (C:31; CP:366).

One of the most moving memories of her childhood relationship with her father is 'On Worms, and Being Lucky'. She remembers his delight on holiday with her find of lugworms at the first attempt:

And he hoicks you up, your Dad, to the space round his head.
You've got the knack, my princess, he says. *You're lucky.*

It's a luck she harnesses to 'lug him back to life' after an operation in old age. 'Yours', she says, 'was the gift to see life gold side up' (SAH:60; CP:338).

'and yettishness'

One poem which balances the dark and the light in life is 'Daffodil Ministry'. It coins the abstract term 'and yettishness' (CP:338) which suggests the quality of being in two minds, of seeing both sides of the argument. The ministry of the title brings together the notion of Quaker ministry and the Romantic notion of the ministry of nature. It is addressing the Wordsworthian concept of the power of nature and poetry in solitary reflection 'when oft in pensive mood' to allay or act as a palliative against the pains of the world. Fanthorpe is irritated by a speaker's line of thought quoted here in the italicised verse

> *O yes, of course the world is harsh,*
> *And suffering, O yes – and yet*
> *This morning as I walked along*
> *And saw the daffodils, I thought –* (SAH: CP:338)

These platitudes are dismissed with irritation as 'daffodilling on' (the formation of a phrasal verb from the common noun suggests a parallelism with 'rabbitting on') and the daffodils themselves are described unlyrically, 'Municipally distributed, like grit'

> Wherever a bulb can lodge and multiply,
> Long-legged, gape-mouthed, a yellow hop in air,
> Daffodils are.

But how, the poem seems to ask, can daffodils provide solace for the world's ills which are even more ubiquitous than in Wordsworth's day: 'Homelessness, poverty, / Injustices, executions, arms trade, war'? (CP:339). And yet the poem ends '*and yet, and yet*' in a very typical undermining of Fanthorpe's certainties.

The comfort of words is, as Carol Ann Duffy suggested in her review, all-important. In the title poem of *Neck Verse* we find this on every level from the comfort of crosswords, to the delight in proverbs, many designed to comfort. 'Word Games', the second section of the title poem, gathers together a lively selection of proverbs from Tyneside, ending with the saying, '*Cheer up hinny, it's nobody's neck*'. This is capped by the gloss, 'But that's not true. It is somebody's neck. / It's mine (NV:58; CP:282-3). The note tells us 'Neck-Verse' was the name given to Psalm 51, so called because it was the trial verse of those who claimed benefit of Clergy. If a condemned person was able to read this verse (originally showing he was ordained, and therefore exempt from trial by a secular court) he had saved his neck. The verse reads:

> Have mercy upon me O God; according to thy loving kindness: according unto the multitude of thy tender mercies blot out my transgressions. Make me to hear joy and gladness that the bones which thou hast broken may rejoice.

Fanthorpe has described this volume as being 'about words and word users' (Wainwright,1995:70) and she makes this clear in the poem 'Awkward Subject': 'Words are my element' (NV:59; CP 283). Many poems testify to the solace of words, of reading and writing.

In her most recent collection *Queueing for the Sun* (2003) she returns to this theme in such poems as 'The Gaoler's Story'. Fanthorpe has a great empathy with prisoners, and has explained a longing:

> above all things to be a prisoner. I imagine this as a life where you don't make choices, where the pattern of life is plain and involuntary. Life in depression is like this anyway but it retains the illusion of choice' (Open Mind, 1997: 21).

In this poem she thinks of Boethius. When deprived of books in prison he writes his *Consolation*.

The gaoler is sceptical:

> Now that's a queer thing. Who would console you,
> In jug, everything lost, disgraced? (CP:421)

For Boethius it is philosophy that provides the consolation 'a high class dame / Who ticks him off for being in the blues, / For listening to Poetry and all that stuff' (Q:15; CP: 421). The poem also records Boethius' last act of generosity and thoughtfulness to his gaoler in getting him out of the prison to spare him the sight of his gruesome death.

> He knew what was coming. How I don't know.
> One morning gave me what he had, and the papers
> (*Hand'em to the future*, he said. The old joke) (CP:421)

The gaoler realises this was an act of love.

Fanthorpe takes comfort from other writers too: from Hopkins whose journals reveal, he has 'all the room in the world' for '*simple people* who have hands to build/ and eyes to see, who open gates' (AWB:21; CP:201); from other diarists such as Samuel Pepys and Gilbert White. Only in a world which brings monstrous deaths to our screens daily can the deaths narrated by them, referred to in Fanthorpe's poem 'The Comforters', be read as comforting – deaths 'Not in the monstrous/ Nuclear glare, but in moderate / Darkness and light, darkness and light / That were the evening and the morning / Of the first ever day (NV:16; CP: 251). She admires the way these diarists 'watched each minute instant so hard / That it broke and flowered into ever' NV16; CP:251). The epigraph to this poem is taken from St John's Gospel: 'The night cometh, when no man can work' (John, 9.iv). Writing is work, is comfort. Of her own work she has commented, 'In order to write I have to concentrate. And concentration is a form of love' (Wainwright, 1995:70).

Idylls

The light in Fanthorpe's work comes from her celebration of the many different manifestations in the human story of love and friendship; she's an archivist of domestic joy, the joy of creativity and the love of language. Her 'Idyll' pictures 'blackbirds, in a late March evening, / Blur of woodsmoke, whisky in grand glasses, / ... A cat materialised on a knee' and a state of mind in which 'All fears of present and future / Will be over, all guilts forgiven' (NV:33; CP:263). But most of all it's a scene in which two people share the writing and reading of poetry. There is a sense that the act of writing is in itself a significant act. At its best it enlightens both writer and reader. It is an act of attention. It is simultaneously special but part of the daily fabric of life. As Fanthorpe says in 'Of Mutability', dedicated to fellow poet Meg Peacocke who was working at the time on her remote smallholding in Cumbria:

> ... the finite scenes
> Of birth and death recur. But things done,
> Meals cooked, fires lit, trees planted, words said,
> Poems observed, have their own posterity. (AWB: 63; CP: 235)

It is very much the sharing of a domestic and intellectual life that is portrayed in the love poetry. These are scattered throughout her collections. Possibly the best known and most anthologised of these poems has been 'Atlas' which takes a deliberately impersonal and ungendered voice to talk about 'the sensible side of love' the implication being of course that there are other sides:

> There is a kind of love called maintenance
> Which stores the WD40 and knows when to use it
>
> Which checks the insurance and doesn't forget the milkman.
> (SAH:339; CP:339)

It progresses from an extensive list of practicalities to the heroic, to a kind of love which is more than the sum of the previous parts which 'upholds / The permanently rickety elaborate / structures of living; which is Atlas.'

'The Absent-Minded Lover's Apology' (SAH:63; CP:340) is one of her more formal love poems, a very Fanthorpian take on E.B.Browning's 'Sonnets from the Portuguese' ('How do I love thee? Let me count the ways'). Fanthorpe presents a series of couplets, each trying to outdo its predecessor in originality, wit and extravagance. Each couplet stretches its lines that bit further to contain its simile, contrasting the formality of this courtly pattern with the domesticity of its images, and the appropriateness of the comparisons for this particular lover. The images seem intended to bring to mind shared experiences: she loves '*warmly* ... *Resourcefully* ... *extravagantly*': each adverb or adverbial phrase is illustrated by a carefully chosen simile:

> I would like you to think I love you *accurately*
> Like Baskerville kern that fits its place to a T
> I would like you to think I love you *with hurrahs* and *hallelujahs*
> Like dog whippetting at you down the intricate hillside
>
> I would like you to think I love you *pacifically and for ever*
> Like collared doves on the whitebeam's domestic branch
> I would like you to think I love you *chronically*
> Like second hand solemnly circumnavigating the clock.

I had read the punch couplet at the end, 'And O I want to love you, not in the absent tense, *but in the here and the now* / Like a present-minded lover' (CP:341) as an indication that Fanthorpe is writing from what she refers to elsewhere as 'the unfocused landscape / of exile' (CP:219); her writer's residency means she is absent from the shared domestic life invoked in this poem, but Rosie insists this is not about physical absence, but absent-mindedness; about a lover who fails to concentrate properly on the loved one. The strange syntax; not, 'I love you warmly', but 'I would like you to think I love you warmly', indicates a wish to offer exactly the sort of love that is needed, to meet expectations, but also an acknowledgement that this needs to be demonstrated in person.

Fanthorpe's 'Going Under' (NV:30; CP:261) is one of the more intimate poems, a sensitive first person delineation of the dynamic between a specific insomniac whose partner 'slips into sleep as fast/ And neat as a dipper'. She is rescued from sleeplessness when 'Out lobs / A casual, heavy arm' to anchor her.' The personal pronoun here is not gendered which makes it easy for readers to recognise and relate to this situation where one partner is lying awake troubled by 'all the things I ever did wrong' and listening to the other's breathing. The title implies simultaneously a sense of sinking into despair, 'Exhausted by guilt', sinking into the arms of a loved one, and sinking into sleep, an anaesthetic both desired and feared.

The grid reference in the title of 'Love Poem OS 759934' (14.2.96) relates to the Ordnance Survey map of Gloucester and The Forest of Dean. It pinpoints her home town, Wotton-under-Edge, which becomes the addressee, the 'She' of this poem. In opening 'She is my Corinna, my Lucasta' Fanthorpe is appropriating and subverting a classical tradition in which a male poet addresses his female muse, a woman or a feminised landscape or nation. Here Fanthorpe is eulogising the landscape of home. Corinna was a Greek poet; some place her as a companion to Pindar 5thC BC; other scholars suggest she lived earlier. A mythologized version of this woman is the addressee of Ovid's *Amores*, love poems known for their wit and humour and seen by some as 'tongue-in-cheek', possibly responsible for his banishment from Rome. *Lucasta* is the title of the Cavalier poet Richard Lovelace's collection of *Epodes, Odes, Sonnets and Songs* (1649) and it is 'To Lucasta on Going to the Wars' for which he is most remembered. There is a tremendous playfulness about Fanthorpe's poem which manages to coexist with a deeply felt affection. She says of Wotton:

Her favourite scent: a dab of woodsmoke behind the ears.
Haute couture and haute cuisine are not her style.

She is an early riser, watery and echoing;
I love her then. And in the evening, when blackbirds call

it a day.

In all the seasons of every year I love her.
And this seems as good a day as any to say so. (C:38; CP:373)

This poem moves from the classical and courtly resonances of its opening line to a demotic, contemporary register in its closing affirmation. I had initially read this final couplet as covert avowal of love for her partner. I note this poem is not, however, included in *From Me To You: Love Poems* (2007) by Fanthorpe and Bailey. (These poems are arranged alphabetically and not attributed; the preface recalls the similar practice of the 1934 collection by Sylvia Townsend Warner and Valentine Ackland *Whether a Dove or a Seagull*.) It is a poem which raises all those questions that will be explored in the final chapter, of Fanthorpe's relationship as a woman writer of the twentieth and early twenty-first century to a canonical tradition of poetry.

For U. A. Fanthorpe the process of writing a poem is itself a movement out of darkness into light, from uncertainty to illumination, from doubt to affirmation of the power of words and the power of love. In an address to school children she begins by describing an early morning walk with a group of birdwatchers begun in darkness: gradually they began to hear the sounds of birds, then see the shapes of trees and branches and finally the other members of the group:

> Poetry is like that early morning walk for the writer. It begins in darkness; the writer doesn't know what's coming. Gradually an idea takes shape and the senses come into action: the writer begins to hear the sounds of words that belong to the poem, to see the shape of it, to feel the images that belong to it ...sometimes the poet has a guide ... sometimes he has to go alone ... in each case there is this movement forward from dark into light ('Stroud Talk' undated script).

Chapter Five

Acts of Appraisal:

the temperamental outsider

I, like Marvell, am a temperamental outsider. [I] acquired the cast of mind which is always looking for the contrary; and – by what seems to me (but perhaps isn't) a natural progression, to paradox, ambivalence, the antithetical.

(U.A.F. on Andrew Marvell)

In all Fanthorpe's best poems there is a note of self-knowledge, a wry intelligent reflection which resists the cosy ... She is among a select and easily-traceable group of poets who manage to compress human motivation into lyric poetry of great formal clarity. Like Hardy she is also able to seal these human behaviours in the wide sweep of history.

Fiona Sampson: www.towerpoetry.org.uk/poetry.matters/june2005

This final section considers Fanthorpe's distinctive place in contemporary poetry. It reflects on her own views about her relationship to a literary tradition alongside the responses of readers, audiences, editors of anthologies, critics, reviewers and over-viewers of the period. It explores a final paradox: Fanthorpe is a poet who sees herself as an outsider, who speaks for the underdog, the voiceless; who uses subversive strategies; resists orthodox lines and attitudes; rewrites myths; prefers the unauthorised versions of the truth; reverses normal hierarchies of precedence. However, she is the same poet who was the first woman to appear in the King Penguin series with her *Selected Poems* (1986); the first woman nominee for the post of Oxford Professor of Poetry (1994) and one of the main contenders for the laureateship on the death of Ted Hughes in 1999. In other words, this 'outsider' has gained Establishment honours. She became a Fellow of the Royal Society of Literature in 1988; was honoured with a CBE in 2001 and awarded the Queen's Gold Medal for Poetry in 2003. Taught on the 'A' level syllabus, she has become part of the literary canon. However, she has not acquired an 'Establishment' voice.

Ironically, concurrent with her inclusion in the National Curriculum, Fanthorpe appears in a collection of lesbian poetry edited by Lilian Mohin entitled *Not For the Academy* (1999). Fanthorpe has managed to be both marginal and mainstream. How do we locate her work in a tradition of English poetry?

From the outset her poems received favourable critical attention, especially from other poets. Charles Causley recognising a 'new and original voice in English poetry' spoke not only of her 'mercilessly exact yet compassionate eye' but also of her 'obvious technical skill and subtle awareness of the possibilities of language' (SW May/June 1979 cited in Wainwright:76). Peter Scupham, writing for *PN Review*, similarly found *Side Effects* 'one of the most arresting first collections of the last few years: mature, adroit, rich in its textures'. He comments:

She places her considerable technical accomplishments at the service of two worlds: a world of people actual and unique in their chosen or unchosen predicaments, and one of place and historical event brooding beyond and behind the horizons of her human subjects' (*PNR* vol 6/4, 1979).

Alan Brownjohn, writing for *Encounter*, enjoys the way her 'detached observer's eye' is able to 'reshuffle experience in a manner that is at once compassionate and disturbing' (in Wainwright:77). George Szirtes, reviewing her second volume *Standing To* (1982), draws attention to her 'often humorous, often painful stoic wisdom and the ability to juxtapose the past with the present, the mythical with the quotidian' (*Times Literary Supplement* 15/07/83).

However, on examining some supposedly representative anthologies of the poetry of the late twentieth century she is marked by her absence. Morrison and Motion's *Penguin Book of Contemporary British Poetry* appeared in 1982 at a point when Fanthorpe had only produced her first two volumes. This supposedly representative anthology gives a generous selection from the work of 20 poets most of whom had been publishing since the late 60's or early 70's. It's worth noting that only five of them are women. Fanthorpe's work would certainly exemplify what the editors pinpoint in their introduction as hallmarks of the contemporary ... the poet as 'onlooker ... dramatist, storyteller' (p12). Seamus Heaney, who has by far the largest representation here with twenty pages of poems, is praised for his 'relish of language as something that embodies politics, history, and locality', a comment which could equally have applied to Fanthorpe but she was too new on the poetry scene to make an appearance here.

In the 80's Fanthorpe consolidated her reputation with her *Selected Poems*, published simultaneously by Peterloo Poets in hardback and King Penguin in paperback in 1986. It drew on her first three volumes, including *Voices Off* (1984). John Mole comments that the best poems in that third collection were 'evocations of particular places, rooted in history which have become palimpsests where the "voices off" are the past generations heard in the fragments that remain' (*Encounter* July/Aug 1985 reprinted in Mole, 1989:108). The *Selected* became a set text for A level students. Linda Anderson saw in this volume 'movement between power and restraint' and particularly enjoyed those poems 'which situate us at the edge of literature allowing "difference" to open up perspectives, questioning formality with colloquial informality' (*Writing Women* Vol. 4 no2).

It was quickly followed by *A Watching Brief* (1987) which, as Roy Fuller points out, contains 'poems which are not only the fruit of observation but also about the value of observation – observation so accurate that it becomes a intellectual and emotional exercise, not least in the setting down' (*The Spectator* 30/1/1988). Lawrence Sail recognised in this volume:

> renewed evidence of her particular gifts of empathy and ventriloquism ... a witness whose honesty and scrupulousness are beyond doubt. Like Carol Ann Duffy she can assume others' voices with complete conviction (*Stand* Summer 1989: 78).

Peter Forbes cites the poem 'Dear Mr Lee' as one which 'encapsulates U.A.Fanthorpe's defence of the ordinary human response against academicism and the encroachments of our late-20th century media-mangled sensibility' (*The Listener* 25/2/1987).

By the time we reach the early nineties with the publication of *Neck-Verse* critics such as Lawrence Sail find 'further evidence of her deftness and ability quietly to surprise':

> Her poems have a sharp awareness of the shortcomings of the contemporary world and the way in which its evasions are mirrored in language ... In this book death and darkness are principals. The poet describes herself too as 'older and more frightened'. The most impressive work in the book engages with the nature of that fear, with 'the black bristly air of darkness' which is composed partly of what is to come, but also of the past. Those poems which test the ground at the edge of the abyss are the book's real strength: they are very good indeed (Sail in *Stand*, Spring: 1993 79-80).

Anne Born compares Fanthorpe's powers of characterisation to a Rembrandt portrait where the spirit shines through the words:

> Fanthorpe's use of language is so masterly that it becomes unobtrusive with its tight economy, hardly any rhyme, its quiet music and unerring choice of words ... Surely no poet writing now can match her for clarity and charity' (*Envoi* 103 Autumn 1992).

Given this range of critical acclaim, it is very disappointing for Fanthorpe not to feature in the next representative anthology of English poetry, Bloodaxe's *The New Poetry*, 1993 edited by Michael Hulse, David Kennedy and David Morley. Whereas before the problem was being too new, now the problem was being too old. The selectors only considered poets born after 1940. This decision worked against many well-established poets including those women like Fanthorpe who came to writing relatively late in life.

The poet and critic Sean O'Brien, discussing this anthology in the preface to *The Deregulated Muse* (1998), his essays on contemporary British and Irish poetry, notes Fanthorpe's exclusion. He comments on the impossibility of a comprehensive account of contemporary poetry in a period marked by a great democratisation of writing. Her work might well have been included in O'Brien's opening chapter 'The Ends of England' which deals with the attitudes to England and nature in the poetry of Larkin, Hughes and Hill. It is astonishing how critics focus so exclusively on male poets when considering the British tradition of landscape poetry. Edward Picot's *Outcasts from Eden: Ideas Of Landscape In British Poetry since 1945* is a prime example which considers not a single woman poet. The idea of the male poet feminising nation and landscape and turning it into a muse is seen as a legacy of the romantic tradition which leaves the woman poet 'struggling for representation in a poetic system that saw her as mute' (Homans,1980:8). It is hard for contemporary women poets to counter, but they have done so.

Eavan Boland has been one of the most articulate about these problems of a woman entering what is perceived as a male tradition where the muse and nation are feminised. In her essay 'The Woman

Poet: Her Dilemma' she deliberately echoes Virginia Woolf when she dramatises the presence of internalised censorious male voices preventing her capturing the immediacy of the poetic moment, which for her is suburban and domestic (Boland, 1996: 239-41). Fanthorpe, as I have explored in detail in chapter three, has a lot to say about England and about the way landscape inscribes people's lives. Her love poem to Wotton (discussed in the previous chapter) is a joint challenge to the masculine hold on the love lyric and the landscape poem.

Fanthorpe gets only one further mention in O'Brien's study. This comes in Chapter Five 'Redressing the Balance' which concerns itself with contemporary women poets. Its main focus is on the work of Adcock, Rumens and Duffy. But in a book where five out of the seven sections deal exclusively with male poets the balance is not exactly redressed. When Fanthorpe *is* mentioned she is grouped with other older women poets: Elma Mitchell, Elizabeth Bartlett and Jenny Joseph who share, as he says, 'common ground in the study of life as it is lived, and suffered, in the everyday world. Their ultimate concern is with people.' He sees them all as 'formal pragmatists', and then goes on to say in a comment very much at odds with other critical opinion and my own readings of these poets:

> They do not seem especially curious about form, voice, perspective or the status of language, a fact which may account for their 'friendliness' to readers uneasy with much modern poetry (O'Brien 1998:155).

It is true that Fanthorpe regretted the way Ezra Pound and the modernists lost the common reader in making poetry difficult. She is considerate of her reader; but nonetheless voice, form, language and perspective are, in my experience, key to any reading of Fanthorpe's work.

In some critical overviews of late twentieth century British poetry Fanthorpe gets no mention at all. It's not surprising that this is the case in David Kennedy's *New Relations: The refashioning of British Poetry 1980-94*, designed as it was to accompany *The New*

Poetry. Her work would however exemplify many of the features of the contemporary which Kennedy defines: a poetry which gives a voice to previously excluded or marginalised constituencies; a poetry aware of the political history of language; poetry as an act of resistance producing counter-structures or counter-narratives; a poetry very much aware of its locations, origins and voice; a poetry that demonstrates a quality of focussed attention ... he quotes Douglas Dunn 'What it comes down to is the love and concern which poetry bestows on its subjects' (from Kennedy's opening chapter 'Voice and Ownership') again a comment that would be highly applicable to Fanthorpe. Nor does she get a mention in Neil Corcoran's *English Poetry Since 1940.* Like many overviewers of the period, he corrals women poets into one small chapter, here Chapter 15 'A Pen Mislaid: Some Varieties of Women's Poetry'.

Antony Thwaite's *Poetry Today: A Critical Guide to British Poetry 1960-1995* likewise has a chapter entitled 'Some Women' which he admits to being a lazy ploy, but Fanthorpe is one of the few women poets to escape this treatment: she is dealt with in the previous chapter alongside several male poets including Andrew Motion and her mentor Vernon Scannell. Thwaite refers to him as 'robustly contemptuous of any literary discourse that smells of the academy' and sees Fanthorpe's poetry sharing his qualities: 'humane, colloquial, honest, demotic, elegiac, accurate, humorous often eloquent ... What they share is a sense of a poem as a well-made object, something made by a truth-teller, won from experience' (Thwaite, 1996: 131).

Notably Fanthorpe does get a place in *The Oxford Book of English Verse* (1999) edited by Christopher Ricks, which covers seven centuries of verse; she is one of only four twentieth century women included.

Women's anthologies – role models

Despite initially disguising her gender, once established as a poet Fanthorpe has fortunately allowed herself to be anthologised in collections of women's poetry and is situated to the fore of the rise of women poets in the final quarter of the twentieth century. Julia Copus, for example, commented in 1996: 'Women poets publishing today are the second generation, so to speak. This means not only that the hardest part of the fight has been won for us, but that we have role models where our role models had none' (*Poetry Review* vol.86, no 4, Winter 1996/7pp 4-24).

The poet and editor Carol Rumens gave Fanthorpe a prominent position at the start of her anthology *Making for The Open*, controversially subtitled *Post-feminist Poetry* (1985 & 87). Peter Childs in his overview of twentieth century poetry discusses Fanthorpe's work only in the context of this 'excellent anthology' which he sees as 'a valuable political gesture which forcefully demonstrated the omissions of the recently published Morrison and Motion anthology' (Childs, 1999:165). Rumens selected three of Fanthorpe's poems with a male subject, 'The Passing of Alfred', 'Father in a Railway Buffet' and 'The Constant Tin Soldier'. Rumens commented in her introduction that the notion that women can write only about women was deeply abhorrent to her. As editor she was emphasising the literary quality of the work of the 'Women Poets' gathered under its cover:

> At the time when *Making For The Open* was first conceived there was no anthology, to my knowledge, of women poets which presented its writers as central to a literary tradition ... Needless to say the conventional anthologies continued largely to ignore all women poets, traditionalist and feminist alike. The feminists were in a slightly more favourable position, having found their own publishing outlets and market. But few people were listening to the woman poet who felt herself to be primarily a poet – one who was confident of her part in the tradition; who while cheered by role-models, felt she could quite happily learn from writers of either gender. This kind of woman has always had a hard time making herself heard.
> (Rumens 1987: xvi)

The comment is particularly pertinent to Fanthorpe. This anthology places Fanthorpe alongside poets not just from England but from America and Europe including Anna Akhmatova and Bella Akhmadulina both of whom feature in Fanthorpe's list of favourite poets. When asked who she admired among women writers the answer was 'On the whole it's the Russians. The second wife of Yevtushenko, Akhelmedulina. She wrote a marvellous poem called 'Rain'. Ahkmatova too' (Pitt, 1994:13. See also the questionnaire for the A level English magazine September 2000: 70.)

Fanthorpe's interest in Ahkmatova was mentioned at the end of chapter two but a wider interest in European writing can be seen in her 1995 review of Stevie Krayer's translation of Rilke's *The Book of Hours*. Fanthorpe refers to this as:

> A book 'concerned with the great distresses of our day, faith and its loss, the need to create, the misery of people in cities, the neglected poor. And the great moving spirit of the Book of Poverty and Death, Francis of Assisi, is one who, because of his powerlessness and love, our cynical age still recognises as holy. What she [Krayer] has unearthed for us is a poem that seems to have been written for us now, at the corner of time where we live.

She quotes Rilke in a letter to Tsvetayeva:

> We touch each other. With what? With beat of wings,
> With distances themselves we touch and meet (p393).

Fanthorpe finds this poem reaches out and touches something in her sensibility across time, across cultures and across gender divides and I am sure that this sense of touching and meeting individual readers through her own poetry, as she does, would mean more to Fanthorpe than any amount of critical acclaim.

Fanthorpe has also enjoyed the work of the American poet Adrienne Rich, born in the same year 1929. She sees her as:

> a very adventurous poet who has opened up the territory for a great many women writers ... It is a great help for a woman, therefore an outsider poet, to find another one somewhere out there who is speaking out for herself and other writers'. (Pitt,1994:13)

In the Rumens anthology Rich is represented by her poem 'Dialogue' which explores exactly the sort of ambivalence and doubleness in thinking about one's sense of self that Fanthorpe is interested in and also appropriately poems from her sequence 'For a Russian Poet'.

It was Rich who, in her seminal essay 'When We Dead Awaken: Writing as Re-vision'(1971), challenged 'the sacredness of the gentlemanly canon' and called not only for the retrieval of 'buried works by women' but also asked contemporary writers to ask their own womanly questions. She defined re-vision as:

> the act of looking back, of seeing with fresh eyes, of entering an old text from a new and critical direction (in Rich 1993:167).

This is ground that Fanthorpe has thoroughly explored, and many critics see this as essentially the territory of the woman poet. Liz Yorke, in her study *Impertinent Voices: Subversive Strategies in Contemporary Women's Poetry* (1991), comments on the potential for re-visionary mythmaking to carry suggestive possibilities for the construction within culture of an alternative field of identification, inviting a new attitude or exploring a fresh perspective on 'real-life women' (15). 'It involves the important task of bringing what has been silenced into speech, but even more crucial is the trans-formation of language itself. In defining her readership as female ... the woman writer has enabled herself to write free of the spectre of male judgement' (Yorke, 1991:17). Yorke states from the start that she is treating women's poetry as a distinctive genre albeit 'inclusive and wide-ranging' (Yorke 1991:11).

It was in the introduction to one of the first anthologies to give individual women poets a generous representation, *The Bloodaxe Book of Contemporary Women Poets* (1985) that editor Jeni Couzyn brought together comments from Roethke to Summerfield illustrating patriarchal attitudes to and negative assumptions about women poets. This synthesis and commentary gives one of the clearest indications of the problems of the exclusion of women poets from the centre of English literature.

By 1993 Linda France was in a position to edit for Bloodaxe *Sixty Women Poets*, a response to the supposedly representative Bloodaxe Anthology *The New Poetry* which included only 17 women out of 55 poets selected. This anthology situates Fanthorpe alongside three generations of women poets born between the early twentieth century (E.J.Scovell is the oldest represented here) and the early 1960's (poets such as Jackie Kay and Eva Salzman.) The poems are arranged alphabetically and Fanthorpe is represented by three very different poems, which illustrate her wit and humour 'Not My Best Side', the satirical 'Poet's Companion', as well as her more elegiac and celebratory 'Fanfare'.

They illustrate the editor's comment on the women writers 'acceptance of contradictions ... the experience of paradox ... For a woman, whatever the gender of the muse, the process of responding openly to and interacting with her imagination is as redemptive as it is imperative.' France sees the 'many different pitches of women's poetry ... that they are skilled in irony and parody, that humour is part of the new openness.' She observes that 'many choose to make use of traditional form to forceful effect, while still managing to make of it something new.' She sees in them an active principle of 'adventure, curiosity and exploration' (18). Many of these qualities are exemplified in Fanthorpe's poetry.

France points out that 'it has long since been unnecessary to justify an anthology of women's poetry on grounds of gender alone'; though she is against 'ghettoising and separatism' she regrets it will continue to be necessary to produce such anthologies 'while women poets are unfairly represented in mixed gender "canonical" anthologies' (France 1993:14). Her anthology has become a classic and illustrates the range and diversity of women's poetry from 1971 to the date of publication.

If anthologies will be used as a register of the contemporary climate then Germaine Greer's analysis of recent anthologies of women poets identifies an unspoken consensus that places U.A. Fanthorpe alongside E. J. Scovell, Elma Mitchell, Elizabeth Bartlett, Patricia Beer, Anne Stevenson, Fleur Adcock, Eileen Ni Chuilleanin, Eavan Boland, Wendy Cope and Selima Hill as major figures of their generation. The critic Jane Dowson, however, adds a warning in her essay 'Older Sisters are Very Sobering Things' (*Feminist Review* no 62 1999: 17) that sufficient studies need to be written to support their achievements to save them from Greer's prediction that hundreds of good women poets 'will be called minor, and forgotten' (Greer 1995:424).

Fanthorpe herself has been a very significant influence in opening up the territory for the current generation of women poets in England. Maura Dooley pays tribute to Fanthorpe as one of several fine poets who have 'created the current happy climate for women writing, reading and publishing today'. She describes the new generation of poets she features in *Making for Planet Alice* as 'inheritors' (Dooley 1997:14). Fanthorpe's own work was brought to light through a National Poetry competition. Now she is the one who is frequently asked to be the arbiter of poetry competitions. In 2007 she and R.V. Bailey were judges of the Mslexia Competition. (They had much to praise but regretted the lack of wit.) Invited to endorse a recent anthology, *Images of Women by Contemporary Women Poets*, Fanthorpe is pleased to acknowledge in her preface the breadth of experience covered in the poems: 'everything is here, and the picture is of a warm and rich humanity, not an embattled gender protest' (Schneider and Wood, 2006: 3).

A separate tradition?

The notion of a separate tradition of women's poetry is disputed territory. As Anne Stevenson explains at the beginning of a 2006 review of the poetry of Fanthorpe, Rumens and Satyamurti:

> Sixty-five years ago the idea that a woman's line in English-language poetry could be established independently of what Eliot simply called 'The Tradition' excited the opposition of the young Elizabeth Bishop, who ... already feared that a gender split between women's and men's poetry would demean and ultimately undermine the foundations of her

art. There is poetry, and there are men and women whose creative gifts demand that they write it. The tradition remains for all poets to learn from and how they modify or 'modernise' it is a personal matter, irrespective of sex (Stevenson in *London Magazine* December 05 / January 06:115).

Stevenson however goes on to comment that the development of poetry in the twentieth century in the hands of 'many gifted women' has been 'more interesting and original than Bishop anticipated'. She sees their achievement as 'a cultural sea-change, a shift of values that challenge the 'high art' of the modernists'. This I would endorse, but worry that her equation of 'women's poetry' with 'the warm accessibility [she] see as "feminine" in a great deal of free verse written by women in the last thirty years' could be exactly the sort of demeaning remark that Bishop feared. She modifies this by acknowledging there is no sign of 'gush or sentimentality' and that these women seem 'readier than many contemporary male poets to undertake major themes which do not shy away from the mysteries of life and death' (ibid:116).

Much darker notes come into Fanthorpe's work from the 1990's on, with *Neck-Verse* and *Safe As Houses* (1995). This added depth does not preclude accessibility. This later volume, the only one to be co-published in America and which also featured on the A level syllabus, revisits her war-torn childhood and looks at the instabilities in and threats to home. Helen Dunmore comments on the way 'Siren Song' from this collection is 'like all her best poems a many-layered thing ... This delicate searching play in words is typical of Fanthorpe ... hers is a poetry which reveals more of itself on each re-reading' (*Observer*, May 26 1996:16).

This textured effect is emphasised too by Guy Wareing, reviewing *Consequences* published five years later (2000). He talks of her

> ability to engage in conversations with the reader ... in a way that seems simple and direct. This creates an illusive simplicity which hides a much deeper, darker voice ... Her deceptively light touch probes the nerve and she is prepared to confront the alien in us.
> (*Poetry Review* 90/3, Autumn 2000: 69-70)

He, like Poetry Book Society selector Kathleen Jamie, is seeing the title sequence as a state of the nation address. But as Maura Dooley says in her Introduction to *Making for Planet Alice*:

> Women are published, read and heard, but their work is not discussed. Until their work is considered and written about consistently, seriously and undifferentiatingly by the major literary journals of the day, their poetry will not have a future as part of the main canon of English Literature (Dooley, 1997:12).

Critical attention

In the gap between *Consequences* and the previous volume some more detailed critical appreciations of Fanthorpe's poetry began to appear not only in England but in Europe and America. Peterloo Poets in 1995 published *Taking Stock: A First Study of The Poetry of U. A. Fanthorpe* by Eddie Wainwright. This considers her work up to *Neck-Verse* with many detailed explorations of individual poems. It usefully appends an interview and extracts from early reviews for which I am indebted. However, I hope that this present study has countered Wainwright's view that 'The poetry of U. A. Fanthorpe does not on the whole deal with the distressing details of contemporary national or world events ... unemployment, wars, famines and so on' (p27).

A typical example of her concerns can be found in the poem 'Reading Between' (CP: 305) – the title refers to reading between the wars, particularly reading between the lines of detective fiction of the period. This poem shows her awareness of the discrepancy between the civilised deaths in these stories that seemed designed 'to gentle the English through war, / And Depression, and war, and peace' and the colossal horrors of deaths in 'Auschwitz, the Burma Road, / Hiroshima, all that followed' (CP:306), which make it hard to return to that 'Never-Never world' with its faith in simple solutions. I have discussed in Chapter Three Fanthorpe's concern with the 'Hundreds And Thousands' of losers in wars, the common soldiers and the innocent civilians whose lives were wasted in the past and continue to be wasted today in our own century which seems not to learn from the past, 'an age / in serious debt to statistics' (CP: 358). Fanthorpe's historical perspective informs her reading of today's civil wars and political instabilities. She's all too aware that '*Atrocity* is what we haven't got used to yet' (CP:384) in a poem that links, through its aggressive metaphors, the greed of developers with the root causes of war.

Kathleen Bell's short monograph for Leicester University in their Bookmark series (1996) begins with an examination of the idea of order in Fanthorpe's poems: 'While order can be used to bestow dignity, it can also be used to threaten or diminish.' Bell looks at the influence of history, particularly the way 'Fanthorpe works against versions of history that sanitise the past' (p8) and the way Fanthorpe 'refuses the conventional voice of authority', how her occasional appearances 'align her securely with the most disturbed and endangered subjects of her poetry' (p9).

Ingrid Rosenberg's 'De-constructing a Poem deconstructing a myth' (published in Germany) is a detailed study of 'Not My Best Side', a response to Uccello's *St George and the Dragon*. She places Fanthorpe in a European tradition of iconic poetry that reaches back to Greek and Roman Antiquity. In a footnote to this scholarly article she lists numerous examples of this genre from the Romantic period to the early 20th century including Eliot's 'La Figlia Che Piange' and Auden's 'Musée de Beaux Arts' (Rosenberg, 1994: 63-75).

Fanthorpe, as Sean O'Brien points out, is a writer 'for whom classical resemblances come instantly to hand' and whose 'other sustaining music is the Bible's.' He suggests that 'the authority and succour of these sources are threatened by a world that no longer shares them and by daily friction and mess' (*Sunday Times Culture* 01/01/2006: 48). Fanthorpe is one of eight poets discussed in Rowena Fowler's study of the presence of Vergil in contemporary poetry in English.

A totally different approach to her work is taken by Lidia Vianu, Professor of Contemporary British Literature at the English Department of Bucharest University. Interviewing Fanthorpe in 2002, she sees her as one of several 'Desperado poets', a term coined with humour to oppose the duller 'postmodernism' in relation to the contemporary. It suggests writers 'who use ... all literary tricks ever devised, in order to be different, to shock at all costs' (http://lidiavianu.bleu.ro/ua_fanthorpe.htm). These 'desperados' become their own trend'. I doubt that Fanthorpe would be totally comfortable with this (or any other) label.

Paul Delaney, an American academic who sees Fanthorpe as 'a dazzling wordsmith' points out that her 'attentive listening to ordinary voices has deep roots in the Christian tradition' (Delaney 1997:327). He later comments:

> her awareness of her own incapacities and awkwardnesses enables her to enter empathetically into others' experience ... The truth Fanthorpe reaches into in her hospital poems has to do with the human worth of the marginalised' (Delaney 1998:6).

There is mention at the end of this study of plans for a *Collected Poems*. However just as Fanthorpe was receiving some wider critical attention, her earlier volumes were going out of print. It felt as if a *Collected* was long overdue. But at the end of the millennium Peterloo Poets was struggling. The business had moved from a cottage industry based in the publisher's dining room to a converted Chapel in Calstock, a stressful procedure of dealing with Lottery bids and builders. But whereas the floor area of the business multiplied by a huge factor, the staffing didn't. Both Harry and Lynn Chambers had suffered serious health problems during this period and Lynn's untimely death early in 2000 was not only a great personal loss to Harry, Lynn's family and many dear friends, including U.A., but also a great loss to Peterloo Poets. Fanthorpe's millennium volume *Consequences* bore an additional dedication 'in memory of Lynn Chambers'. Lynn was a larger than life character with a generous spirit, a great sense of humour, an erudite wit and a great belly laugh. She modestly worked in the background in a way that in retrospect seems heroic. Lynn had played a very full part in this family business. Whereas large publishing firms have separate departments to deal with submissions, editing, distribution, publicity and the nitty-gritty of typesetting, choosing book covers, seeing books through the printing process, grant applications, permissions, financial reports, tax returns, royalties, Harry and Lynn were all these departments rolled into one with the help of one reliable office worker and occasional casual staff to stuff things in envelopes. So there was a delay.

Collected Poems 1978-2003

An eighth volume, *Queueing for the Sun*, appeared in 2003. It was selected by Antony Thwaite for the *Sunday Telegraph*'s 'Books of the Year' feature, commended by him as 'an interesting retrieval of bits of the past, wry, funny, original. Her poems have a cutting edge that is sharp without being cruel.' By then even the *Selected Poems* was out of print. U.A. had been very loyal to her publisher. When the long-awaited *Collected Poems* arrived in 2005 there would have been a real sense of celebration and achievement for both the poet and the Press. The different images on the covers of the hardback and the paperback edition reflect two polarities of her concerns. The hardback features Van Gogh's *Still Life With Books* (*Les Livres Jaunes*); the paperback has a lively animated domestic scene of *Washing Up* by Sir Stanley Spencer.

Sean O'Brien in his review of Fanthorpe's *Collected Poems* points out that 'Fanthorpe has sometimes been treated as slightly cosy, but the evidence reveals a tough-minded compassion, dealing with the facts' (*Sunday Times Culture* 01/01/2006).

Stevenson's review cited earlier is predominantly positive but it accuses Fanthorpe of being too prosaic 'more Dorothy than William'. The assumed value judgements in that comment should be questioned. Dorothy Wordsworth's journal writing is now valued for its own sake and not simply for the light it throws on the more famous brother's writing. When Fanthorpe lifts lines of Dorothy's prose, and embeds them in her poem it illustrates the vividness of the imagery. A good example is when she quotes the footnote to Dorothy's journal entry for April 4th 'N.B. Deer in Gowbarrow Park like skeletons' from which she takes the title of her poem (CP: 194). This phrase offers not only a striking image (a significant detail overlooked by William when he trawled this entry for his own poem) but also a phrase interesting for its rhythm and stresses. When Fanthorpe reiterates that injunction 'N.B., N.B.' it is intended to draw our attention to how well Dorothy notes the details that matter, what an observant and poetic eye she has. In an interview for *The National Poetry Archive* Fanthorpe said:

> Prose is all right but it's a young brother compared to poetry. It didn't begin to exist until well on in the career of poetry. Poetry has all the voices – wit, sincerity, pastiche, tragedy, delight, and most importantly it's with us from the start of our lives to the end: at the start of our lives, with lullabies and mothers crooning to babies, at the end of our life, with hymns over a grave. It's there all the time, and for the biggest moments of all.

And yet Fanthorpe is someone who also values the economy and directness of good prose and can tell when it has poetic potential. Critic Neil Powell picks up on the way its qualities are embedded in her poetry in his review of *Neck-Verse:*

> Fanthorpe, too, casts her vote for that prose integrity, which is why her moments of celebration carry absolute conviction, as in 'May 8th: how to recognise it'… hers is a world grown triumphantly beyond any easy delusions of spring . (*The Times Literary Supplement* 20/11/1992)

Fanthorpe is the inheritor of both the Wordsworths' skills. She, like Dorothy, 'approaches the world with curiosity, looking at it, reading books about it, assembling facts and observations, taking notes' (Stevenson, 2006: 120) but in condemning much of Fanthorpe's work as prosaic Stevenson is unable to see its connection with Wordsworth's achievement in recording the language really used by men. Fanthorpe finds poetry in people's words. Especially women's words. Fanthorpe has said that she found she couldn't write polemic about women and sees herself 'not as a woman writer, but as finding an audience of women and saying things women would understand' (Hacker, 1989:163).

Fanthorpe explains to Angela Pitt that she went over to writing about women towards the end of *Voices Off* and throughout *A Watching Brief*:

> 'That's when it hit me that women were so interesting to write about because there was so much suppressed' (Pitt, 1994:13).

She gives the example of 'Unauthorised Version':

> Mary and Martha being sisters might conceivably have had the sort of relationship my mother had with my Aunt. I thought it would be fun to see what happened if I interpreted the relationship in the light of how they managed, which was understanding without saying. And the idea that Christ wouldn't have understood what they were saying because he wasn't a sister, he was only a man' (ibid).

This is exactly the sort of womanly question Rich was hoping would be voiced. Though done in a playful way, poems like this in turn raise serious questions in the reader's mind about the nature of the authority of the myths and meta-narratives we have been brought up with and their significance in the construction of our own sense of literary, social, cultural location or identity. Jan Montefiore has commented that 'Fanthorpe's take on tradition and myth is many-sided, and not only preoccupied with gender issues (*Poetry Review* 94.2, Summer 2004:65).

Fanthorpe says she had never been given the idea of women as 'A Second Sex', of men being in any way superior to women. She saw it as an advantage in this respect to have been a pupil at an all girls' school, to have studied at a women's college and then to have taught in an all girls' school. A later experience of being on a counselling course at Swansea amongst rugger-playing, male-voice-choir-singing men was a shock she says, 'like having my eyelids forcibly torn off' (Pitt, 1994:13). On the other hand she has made many comments about the social and economic inequalities in society, especially the patriarchal privileging of boys and men in terms of educational opportunities. Her poem 'Kinch and Lack' (CP:365) is a good example.

In a note to Suzanne Raitt who was collecting material for her volume *Volcanoes and Pearl Divers* Fanthorpe confides, 'I suppose I was a woman writer, but I steadily rejected the experiences that I thought of as being women's.' She offers for this collection:

> A chronological autobiographical piece, exploring some of the false moves and mistaken identities that offer themselves to the lesbian and the writer in the search for imaginative truth (1992).

When Fanthorpe was asked by Angela Pitt if she felt part of a tradition Fanthorpe responded:

> I don't feel part of a tradition, because to be a woman poet was almost to be nothing at all ... Even Virginia Woolf felt that she didn't know enough about the classics to be a poet, so what I felt as a great advantage when I started out was the lack of a tradition, in particular that no man had ever been a woman receptionist in a hospital (Pitt, 1994:14).

Fanthorpe did feel she had found a new subject, a new territory which she could validly claim; she had previously felt silenced and muffled, had difficulty finding a confident point of entry into writing. It was only later she became aware that contemporaries such as Connie Bensley and Elizabeth Bartlett (initially also published by Peterloo Poets) had been writing from a similar territory and perspective.

Her resistance to the notion of a woman's tradition of writing may seem surprising given the nature of the poems already discussed and others to be considered in this chapter that directly address or reflect on the lives and work of earlier women writers; there is much in Fanthorpe's writing that establishes a clear matrilineage with other women writers across the centuries and cultures. But the disclaimer is in keeping with responses of many other contemporary women writers who still have to resist being categorised and labelled as 'women poets' or 'feminists', as those labels tend to be dismissive. As Jackie Kay so forthrightly explains:

> when all [people] ever do is define the Other in society, the black person, the gay person, the woman, then they kind of assume by that the white person, the heterosexual and the man are the norm and everybody else deviates from that ... you don't get the likes of Ted Hughes or Andrew Motion constantly being described as white, male, middle class and heterosexual'.
> (In Conversation with Richard Dyer, *Wasafiri* 29, 1999:57)

Different spheres

It is worth noting that Fanthorpe's poems frequently acknowledge the different worlds that men and women inhabit. Just as women's magazines failed to offer 'the golden arena / Of dedicated action ... / Only the impossible junctions of being a woman' (Woman's World' SE: 62); there is a tendency for some to think that women's poetry confines itself to a domestic sphere. Fanthorpe herself has expressed irritation at these assumptions. In a talk given to trainee teachers 'Without Curiosity There Can Be No Literature' she read Kingsley Amis's poem 'Something Nasty in the Bookshop' to point out that the distinction he makes between men and women poets: the men saying 'I travel, I think, I can read' but the 'girls' saying 'I love you!' 'I love you!' 'I love you!' is an old fashioned view of women who now also travel, think and read – not to mention work, as well as love.

Women poets have established the domestic and the maternal as a fit subject for poetry which can be explored in a far from senti-mental or clichéd way. Kate Clanchy's *Newborn* (Picador 2004), a collection of poems in which she attends to the child from conception to infancy is testimony to this. Many women poets have made fine poems negotiating the tension between the 'monstrous selfishness' needed to be a writer and the selflessness needed to be a mother and carer. It is a tension wittily and honestly expressed in poems from widely differing cultural contexts: Kathleen Jamie's poem 'Wee Wifey': ('I have a demon and her name is Wee Wifey') and Jean Binta Breeze's 'Ordinary Mawning' ('wish me never did breed, but Lawd / mi love dem') are two striking examples.

This is not Fanthorpe's territory though she plays teasingly with these assumptions about the woman poet's interests in her poem 'Needle Work' (the penultimate poem in her *Collected Poems* (CP: 467). This is a riddling sonnet, where the needle in the title 'the genius at the heart of things', is not the needle of a seamstress, but of a compass. Not being a mother or wife (in the traditional sense) she is free from some of those demands and interruptions that many women face. Her poem 'The Poet's Companion' (CP: 270), which has come in for some flak from feminist critics, simultaneously satirises the traditional role of the woman in partnership with a male writer, but one suspects embeds some of the attributes of her own supportive partner and shows her own good fortune. Christina Patterson in a profile on Fanthorpe for The Independent commented:

> [U.A.F.] is, ironically enough, probably the only woman poet I can think of who almost literally has a wife ... It was Rosie who encouraged her to write, Rosie who collated the early poems, Rosie who told her which magazines to send them off to, Rosie indeed who posted them (Patterson, 2003:23).

Although Fanthorpe's situation frees her from many of the tensions in the writing lives of her female predecessors she is nonetheless sensitive to problems in the lives of earlier women writers. There are several poems that look at women writers in relation to the men in their lives.

'An easy day for a lady' (SAH: 45; CP: 323) looks at the relationship between Virginia Woolf and her father on a climbing holiday. It illustrates the way the world or sphere of men and women is defined by the way the Alpine climbs are graded: from 'Inaccessible', at the most difficult, to 'easy day for a lady'. For the father, Leslie Stephen, the Alps are 'a clean competitive world.'

> The Alps were right for him. Unpeopled. Snow
> Affirmed no one had ever been that way. (CP:323)

Each peak offers 'New challenges, new hazards, a new route'. The assumption in the guide books is that women would not want such challenges, that they would content themselves with the gentlest slopes.

Interestingly she describes Woolf's writing in terms of mountaineering:

> She risked the lunatic leap between feeling and sense,
> And invented the syntax for it. She charted
> Innominate peaks of silence, emptiness, space.' (CP:324)

Fanthorpe too takes leaps of imagination, takes risks in her writing, is very inventive with structures and forms, charts new territories. In this poem she shows the connection between the observations Virginia made in her early letters and diaries, holidaying with family in Cornwall, travelling with her father in the Alps, and the use made of these experiences in her fiction. 'She watches him. She will use this later.' Movingly the last stanza implies Woolf can almost stand aside and watch her own death:

> She walked to death, prospecting
> The weedy channelled Ouse, that lowland stream,
> Stones in her pocket.
>
> She watches this. Some things are never used.
> (CP: 325)

Except by one's heirs. Perhaps this is one of the many occasions where Fanthorpe becomes a ghost-writer, inhabiting the voice of her subjects who write their story through her. There is empathy here with Virginia's alarm at 'the sheer-drop silences in front of strangers. / Like a hole in the world.' An equation takes place here between the subject and the writer's position of silent observer.

Her poem 'From the Third Storey' takes as its epigraph a conversation between David Plante and Jean Rhys cited in his book *Difficult Women*:

> "You have to be selfish to be a writer."
> "Monstrously selfish?"
> "Monstrously selfish," she said. (VO: 74; CP:178)

The poem goes on to explore the irony of this assertion when testimony shows how so many women writers in fact put other people first. They managed to write what was derogatively referred to as their 'scribbles', in other words their major novels, without privacy, without rooms of their own, subject to many interruptions in the spaces left after 'home duties' were fulfilled leaving them free to enter what Charlotte Bronte refers to as 'her own bright sphere' of writing. Interlaced with these stanzas giving thumbnail sketches of Jane Austen, Charlotte Bronte, George Eliot, Jean Rhys and Virginia Woolf are others in parenthesis, comprising quotations from *Jane Eyre* alluding to 'the moans', the 'snarling, snatching sounds' that come from the third storey at Thornfield where Bertha Mason, the first Mrs Rochester, is incarcerated. As Linda Anderson observes, 'the poem juxtaposes the traditional restraint of the woman writer's life, with the 'mad' voice of repressed power' (*Writing Women* Vol 4 no 2).

The last stanza in italics is taken from Jean Rhys's *Wide Sargasso Sea*. In writing back to *Jane Eyre* Rhys was fulfilling a long commitment to tell the story of 'that particular Creole'. In her prequel she recreates Bertha as the young Antoinette Cosway and the last lines of the poem belong to her when she is just about to set fire to Thornfield and jump to her death:

Now at last I know
Why I was brought here
And what I have to do

These words which can be seen to relate not only to Antoinette but to her creator Jean Rhys, could also be read as Fanthorpe's affirmation of her own belated sense of vocation as a writer.

This poem is just one of many examples of Fanthorpe's use of intertextuality in her work, a common feature of contemporary women poets identified by the poet and critic Deryn Rees-Jones:

> an intertextuality which finds them drawing on texts by both men and women, engaging both with gender politics and the politics of a literary tradition in which – and against which – they write (Rees-Jones, 2005:16).

The intertexts in Fanthorpe's work however are just as likely to come from art history, or philosophy, or mountaineering as from literature or writers' journals. Fanthorpe and Bailey talk about a shared love of reference books:

> not just the big obvious ones like the 24 vols. of the OED and the DNB, but maps (those beautiful things), and reference books of all kinds, dictionaries of slang and surnames and saints, of dialects and diseases and dates. Books of facts: facts about birds and trees and medieval churches and rivers. History, both fictional and true. Books about journeys from *Pilgrim's Progress* to the ascent of K2 (*Acumen 50*, 2004).

It's easy to see how this wider reading informs Fanthorpe's poetry. But she manages to be erudite without being obscure.

A canonical line

Fanthorpe is particularly aware of the differences facing women writers in both the production and reception of their writing. As Jane Dowson observes:

A convincing case can be made that women are able to disrupt poetical norms with an irreverence unencumbered by any nostalgia for a tradition which has ignored them (*Feminist Review* 62 Summer 1999:17).

Yet it is clear that Fanthorpe draws on a rich heritage of a more traditional canonical and predominantly male literary line via the Romantics and Victorians as far back as the Anglo-Saxon Beowulf poet.

In a discussion about Eliot's essay "Tradition and the Individual Talent" Zadie Smith argues against Eliot's assumption that 'personality amounts to simply the biographical facts of ones life'; rather she sees it as 'our way of processing the world, our way of being'. Smith turns Eliot's claim of a devotion to a tradition as a sign of impersonality on its head and claims that 'the choices a writer makes within a tradition ... constitute some of the most personal information we can have about him [sic]' (*The Guardian Saturday Review* 13/01/07: 5). Fanthorpe's preferences are particularly telling.

The poet and critic Tom Paulin has argued about a split tradition in poetry: seeing 'on the one hand a high, melodic, vowel-based tradition which includes Shakespeare, Wordsworth and Eliot which 'looks south to the Romance languages for its essential inspiration' and on the other hand what he refers to as a 'Gothic tradition ... northern and consonantal'. Its roots, he says, are in the people, in an oral culture which produces poems that have 'a fricative, spiky, spoken texture'. This is a tradition that would include Anon and in more recent centuries Clare, Barnes, Browning, Hopkins, Hardy, Frost, and Edward Thomas (Paulin, 1996: 172-3).

I'm not convinced by this distinction and would place Shakespeare and Wordsworth in a list of poets for whom oral culture and voice are important. Fanthorpe's writing is influenced by and fuses elements from both traditions. In addition she brings a woman's perspective to them. She has said she admires Shakespeare, Chaucer and Wordsworth. Although a late recruit to Wordsworth (having been put off him through study at school) he is another poet Fanthorpe admires for his desire 'to keep the reader in the company of flesh and blood' and his attention to marginal characters who 'come out on top' (in Mark and Rees-Jones, 2000:34).

Eliot has been an influence too. From him Fanthorpe got 'the idea of collage, of nonsequiturs, of not spelling things out for the reader.' The influence of his *Four Quartets* can be seen clearly in her 'Consequences' series and Delaney discusses the echo of *The Waste Land* in the final lines of 'Getting It Across':

> In that last line of direct address [And you, and you] the speaker suddenly resorts to an urgently personal appeal. In theatrical terms Fanthorpe breaks the fourth wall. I am reminded of a moment in *The Waste Land* when the speaker turns and transfixes the reader as 'You! hypocrite lecteur! – mon semblable, – mon frère'. (Delaney 1997:337)

However, Fanthorpe has strongest affinities with many in Paulin's second list, the line referred to as 'gothic'.

She says she was lucky enough to be taught Anglo-Saxon the Tolkien way ('this is not philology, it is poetry') and has gained from it not only a fascination for the stories of 'dragons, ruined cities, lost battles, stoic courage' (Acumen 50, 2004) but also a passion for the alliterative line. She says she tries to edit out what she sees as an obsession with this. (One that rightly got away is the opening of 'Superannuated Psychiatrist': 'Old scallywag scapegoat has skedaddled' (CP:272). It is not surprising then that she is also a great admirer of Basil Bunting, a fellow Quaker, whose epic 'Briggflatts' is listed amongst her favourite poems. Written in alliterative and caesuraed lines 'Briggflatts' shows his interest in the musical phrase, the sound qualities as well as the etymologies of words. The world of Briggflatts is:

> a place of historical continuities and to express it Bunting has collated timelessly valid words. His linguistic craft builds up a textual site where words, as thoughts, constitute one transhistorical continuum (Dennis Brown in Day and Docherty, 1997:29).

It is, however, Fanthorpe's appreciation of and response to Browning, which connects her position in a traditional canon with her significance in the rise of women's poetry at the end of the twentieth century:

> Robert Browning is always the one I go back to if I feel I've lost imaginative direction, or the right voice, because he is so endlessly inventive. He's got this marvellous willingness to try anything as far as language is concerned; there's no feeling of propriety or constraint about him (Pitt, 1994:14).

A lot has been said over many years by critics about the importance of the dramatic monologue as a form in the hands of the woman poet. Fanthorpe gave a talk at the South Bank (May 2006) on the influence of Browning on her work. The critic Virginia Blain has commented that it is 'Browning's willingness to explore through dramatization, viewpoints other than that of the conventional bourgeois male' that has endeared him to women writers:

> Dramatic forms offered the opportunity to imitate or inhabit less socially accepted positions without taking direct responsibility for them; with lyric forms, by contrast, poets were too often assumed to be the speaking 'I' of the poem, and in the case of women poets, this readerly assumption was a powerful agent for self censorship. (Blain in Shattock, 2001:177)

The way Victorian poets developed the transgressive properties of this genre has been explored by critic Isobel Armstrong who also discusses this dramatic form as a protection against self-exposure. Laura Severin qualifies this:

> It has the double advantage of allowing the female poet to hide or let the mask slip, as she chooses – even more importantly it allows the woman poet to highlight her cultural context in exposing feminine identity as a role (Severin, 2004: 6).

This study, *Poetry Off the Page: Twentieth Century British Women Poets in Performance*, considers the element of performance 'giving another layer to an already multi-layered work' (ibid:8). Though Severin takes as her contemporary examples Liz Lochhead and Jackie Kay, it is interesting to relate these arguments to the experience of seeing U.A. Fanthorpe in performance. Barbara Baker comments on the 'Double-Act' of Fanthorpe and Bailey: 'their readings are unforgettable; moving and entertaining.' Their formal dress, often in black and white trouser suits with attention to details of colourful cravats and ties announces 'this is our performative selves'. Inevitably their stage presence challenges the audience's assumptions about 'the woman poet'. The argument is developed by Deryn Rees-Jones In *Consorting with Angels: Essays on Modern Women Poets* who points out the monologue's 'potential for multiple ironies ... it seeks to embody the speaker while also saying the presence of this body is *not* the poet's ... the monologue plays with ideas of embodiment and presence representing a movement between self and other' (Rees-Jones 2005:14). Two of Fanthorpe's dramatic monologues feature in the selection of her poetry in Deryn Rees-Jones' companion anthology *Modern Women Poets*. In her introduction she includes Fanthorpe in a long list of women poets who make use of this dramatic form 'which offers a strategic circumvention of any direct equation between poet, poem and poetic 'I' ... a genre which highlights women poets' anxieties about their self-presentation and poetic determination' (Rees-Jones 2005a:19).

Back in 1971, Adrienne Rich who began writing much earlier than Fanthorpe, though they are the same age, commented 'I hadn't found the courage yet to do without authority or even use the pronoun I'. It's not until Fanthorpe's later poems there is less hiding behind masks and more willingness to put herself into the frame, to use 'I', to scrutinise her own attitudes and motives, to adjust her own self-image. What Fanthorpe says she likes most about Browning is that:

he's really sold on people, and basically people are what I'm interested in ... he very rarely describes anything that hasn't got people ... at the heart of it. And the weirdness of people. (Pitt, 1994:14)

In *Poets on Poets* Fanthorpe introduces a selection from the Dorset writer William Barnes. She refers to him as a 'pioneer writer' with a passion for language:

As a poet he wanted to celebrate the language pronunciation and cadences of Blackmore Vale, seeing in them the legitimate historical heirs to Old English, hence the absence of romance words in his work.

She responds both to his subject matter, writing at a time of post-Napoleonic depression and the enclosure movement, and forms:

These intensely *heard* poems, with their obsessive rhymes and metrical sophistication, which Hardy and Hopkins were the first to spot, are also sombre and comic rehearsals of the great themes of rural life: dispossession, labour, spring and fall, love.
(in Rennison and Schmidt, 1997:7)

Barnes, she says, never achieved national fame but 'saw himself as a spokesman for a community undervalued'.

The temperamental outsider

It is in an introduction to a lecture given in 1993 in the Poetry Society's *Poets on Poets* series Fanthorpe's talks about her strongest sense of affinity with the poet Andrew Marvell, whom she sees as a 'temperamental outsider'. She makes some telling comments on this subject:

The poetry of these islands is full of outsiders, right from the start – outsiders because of race and language, like the Welsh or the Irish or the Scots; outsiders because of class – writers like Robert Burns or John Clare; or because of gender – like E.B. Browning. Nowadays we have a flood of writers from overseas, from the West Indies and Africa and India and so on; and some of them are writing about their 'outsider' experiences' – what it feels like to be an outsider.

But all of these are writing as representatives of others like themselves, with whom in some way they belong – they represent other outsiders. They have, as we say, a constituency for whom they speak.

By contrast she defines Marvell as an outsider on the inside:

> He belonged in all the usual ways to the ruling class; and he never abandoned it. He did all the proper things ... Yet he never really belonged ... It's not a matter with him of a difference of race, or class or gender, but a difference of temperament.

> I think my temperament is the same as his ... while there are many poets from whom I've learned, many whom I like, there's only one I feel I share a skin with and that one is Marvell.

She defines particular attitudes which emerge from his work to which she closely relates: his passion for balance, for fairness, for justice. 'You can see this operating in what he says and what he doesn't say – but he never wrote about it directly'; the way poetry mattered to him ... his best friends were poets yet his best work was unpublished in his lifetime; 'he cared greatly about freedom, and about civil rights; he was a man essentially on his own – thinking, and watching, and making provisional assessments – just as perhaps a spy (that quintessential outsider occupation) might do.' She goes on to explain what is at the heart of her sense of connectedness with Marvell:

> All through our childhood, my brother and I were never quite certain that we didn't wear wigs. We were a talkative pair, and our parents, to control the flow a bit, evolved the notion that we were barristers, counsel for the prosecution and counsel for the defence. As a result my father, who was in real life himself a barrister, became the judge. 'Patience, my learned friend' he would rebuke my brother, or 'you have the court's ear' to me.

This way of talking, of thinking, led us both to acquire the cast of mind which is always looking for the contrary; and – by what seems to me (but perhaps isn't) a natural progression, to paradox, ambivalence, the antithetical, whereby it is possible to mean both things as well as neither (pp.6-7).

It is this awareness of the contrary, of paradox, ambivalence and the antithetical that link these two poets and surfaces so often in Fanthorpe's work. It often shapes the structure of ideas in her poems.

The lecture is about the things she'd like to think she'd inherited from Marvell. She comments on Marvell's courtesy: 'Recipients are all relatively helpless unimportant people and things. That's why they matter.' She's interested in the relationship between the private man, the tutor and the public man the MP: 'He watched. He listened. He kept his own counsel ... his peculiar handling of the first person singular. You can never be quite sure who he is. It's safest on the whole to suppose that the one person he is not is himself.' She goes on to admit:

I don't find it easy to write in the first person either. It comes more naturally to me to adopt what I would call a personal myth. And of these personal myths, the major ones are: the sentry; the watcher; the guide or conductor; and the dog Cerberus who guarded the entrance to the classical underworld. These were all present, in one way or another, in my job as hospital receptionist, and – later – as writer-in-residence.

In both of these capacities you watch, listen and think. But you don't belong. Equally you are watched – as no doubt Marvell was at Appleton House – to see if you are doing the right thing, fitting in, earning your keep.

She also expresses fascination with Marvell's alter ego 'The Mower'. Her poem 'The Man who Loved Gardens' is a tribute to Marvell, the man who 'presided with irony / Over sublunary confusions, / Reconciling the irreconcilable / Nature of things with a pun (Q:30; CP:435).

159

Like Marvell she has referred to herself as a spy. Like Marvell, Fanthorpe is simultaneously mainstream and subversive. Vernon Scannell recognises:

> Fanthorpe is an original. Whatever her literary influences may be, they have been so thoroughly assimilated that her voice sounds wholly individual and very English (*Poetry Review* Vol 77/4 Winter 1987/8).

Just as Fanthorpe values idiosyncrasy, eccentricity and warm-heartedness in individuals, so readers value her work for its distinctive voice. Fanthorpe's concern, like Virginia Woolf before her, is for The Common Reader. She is a very popular poet; *Consequences* was featured on Radio 4's *A Good Read* (12/8/03), quite unusual for a volume of poetry to be selected for discussion in this way, and she was also a guest on *Desert Island Discs* (Radio 4 15/5/04). But she doesn't court popularity. Her main focus is on the poem's integrity: 'what I'm really concerned with is getting it right, telling the truth, letting the poem say what it wants to say' (in Hacker, 1989:163). Carol Rumens in her Bloodaxe lecture 'Line, Women and Song' says:

> I am all for poetry as a force of opposition – and as a form of linguistic play. A poem will tend to be both these things qua poem. But I think primarily [poetry] is a truthfully conducted invitation to explore someone else's humanity. Ordering its insights into a pleasure giving pattern (because it is an art form after all) a poem can only finally show us, through language, a human being being human. It gives us his or her self – ideolect, mood, odour, texture, rhythm (Rumens, 2007: 66).

Fanthorpe is 'a connoisseur ... of other people's lives' (CP:162); she does make these lives vivid to the reader, yet 'in all Fanthorpe's best poems there is a note of self-knowledge, a wry intelligent reflection' (Sampson, 2005). What comes across even more clearly in a reading of the *Collected Poems*, is the quality of the poet's attention to the world, a poetic sensibility resistant to 'authorised' versions of reality. Fanthorpe's poetry is as much as anything an act of resistance to those forces, which 'threaten to scupper verbal sensitivity... the depthless, commodified, instantly legible world of advanced capitalism, with its unscrupulous way with signs, computerised communication and glossy packaging of experience' (Eagleton, 2007:17). She resists the sanitisation of the past as much as the commodification of the present. Her poetry puts us in a real world of complex experience, living with contradictions and paradox, understanding the 'andyettishness' of life.

Equally significant is the subtle craftsmanship, the poetry, the living language in which those observations are expressed. Fiona Sampson places her:

> among a select and easily-traceable group of poets who manage to compress human motivation into lyric poetry of great formal clarity. Like Hardy she is also able to seal these human behaviours in the wide sweep of history (www.towerpoetry.org.uk/poetry.matters/june2005).

She is an inheritor of what Paulin refers to as the 'lovely acoustic texture of Hardy's verse ... his passion for the human voice ... his obsessive fascination with sight' (Paulin,1996:180). The heard quality of the poem always matters to her and it is not surprising that several of her poems have been set to music:

> Poetry exists most emphatically in the ear and there is quite a strong resemblance to music. You put in all sorts of subtleties which form a covert pattern. You don't expect people to notice, but these subtleties bind it together in an aural way (in Pitt, 1994: 14).

Fanthorpe's multi-layered poetry, rich in acoustic texture, is the work of a 'temperamental outsider', a truth-seeker who resists the easy answers, who delves into the past to understand the present, who honestly faces tensions of faith and doubt, who witnesses what it is to be human at a particular point in history. This poetry which attends to marginal lands and marginal people also resists easy classification. The *Collected Poems 1978-2003* shows a very talented writer; a woman and a lesbian, locations seen by some as marginal, making a distinctive contribution to the mainstream of an English poetic tradition.

BIBLIOGRAPHY

Select Bibliography

The following books by U.A.Fanthorpe are published by Peterloo Poets unless otherwise stated. Peterloo Poets, The Old Chapel, Sand Lane, Calstock, Cornwall PL18 9QX.

1978   *Side Effects*

1980   *Four Dogs: A poem* (limited edition)

1982   *Standing To*

1984   *Voices Off*

1985   *Selected Poems* 1985, Peterloo Poets (hb); King Penguin (pb) 1986

1985   *The Crystal Zoo* (with John Cotton and L. J. Anderson) Oxford University Press

1987   *A Watching Brief*

1987   *The Bristol Triptych*: A Suite for Speaker, Piano and String Orchestra with words by U.A.Fanthorpe and music by Nigel Dodd (Five poems by U.A.Fanthorpe with five Illustrations by Frank Shipsides published by St George's Music Trust.)

1991   *Mortal Heart* (with Tony Lopez) Spacex Literature

1992   *Neck-Verse*

1994   *Painter and Poet: Three Poems* (with wood engravings by Simon Brett) Prospero Poets

1995   *Safe As Houses* Peterloo Poets and Story Line Press, USA

2000   *Consequences*

2002   *Christmas Poems* (with Enitharmon Press)

2003   *Queueing for the Sun*

2004   *Collected Poems 1978-2003*

2006   *Homing In: Selected Local Poems* (with an Introduction and illustrations by R.V. Bailey) The Cyder Press, Gloucester

2007   *From Me to You: Love Poems by U.A. Fanthorpe and R.V. Bailey* Peterloo/ Enitharmon

U.A.Fanthorpe's work has appeared in many anthologies including:

Carol Rumens (ed.), *Making for the Open: Post-Feminist Poetry*, London, Chatto (1985 - revised 1987)

Barabara Blenheim (ed.), *Five Modern Poets*, Harlow, Longman, 1993

Penguin Modern Poets 6, 1996 (Appears alongside Charles Causley and Elma Mitchell)

Paul Jordan, *Three Contemporary Poets* (with Glyn Wright and Grace Nichols) London, Hodder and Stoughton, 1997

Linda France (ed), *Sixty Women Poets* Newcastle, Bloodaxe, 1993

Lilian Mohin (ed) *Not for the Academy: Lesbian Poets*, Onlywomen Press, 1999

Deryn Rees-Jones (ed), *Modern Women Poets* Newcastle, Bloodaxe, 2005

Myra Schneider and Dilys Wood (eds.), *Images of Women by Contemporary Women Poets*, Arrowhead Press, 2006

Carol Ann Duffy (ed) *Answering Back: Living poets reply to the poetry of the past*, Picador, London, 2007

Miscellaneous essays, forewords, critical writings

Foreword to *Sauce: The Poetry Virgins*, edited by Linda France, Bloodaxe, 1994

Rennison, N & Schmidt, M. (eds) *Poets on Poets*, Carcanet/ Waterstones, 1997 (UAF introduces the work of William Barnes)

Dymock: The Time and The Place, The Laurie Lee Memorial Lectures No. 3, The Cyder Press, University of Gloucestershire, (delivered at The Cheltenham Festival, October 2001) 2002

Preface to *Images of Women by Contemporary Women Poets* edited by

Myra Schneider and Dilys Wood, Arrowhead Press, Darlington, 2006

Unpublished essays and prose pieces (scripts from lectures)

Lecture on Andrew Marvell (Poetry Society's *Poets on Poets* series, Bradford 2/12/1993)

Lecture on Browning (Poetry Society's 'Under The Influence Series' 18/05/2006)

'Words at the end of their tether' (WAET)

'Without curiosity there can be no literature' (WCNL)

'An Honest Trade' undated (AHT)

'The Uses of Ignorance' (TUOI) (Swanwick Writers' Summer School 1993)

'A Scrappy Little Harvest' (ASLH)

'Autobiography of a Reader' (1984 AOR)

'War at Whitstable' (WAW)

Waiting Gentlewoman revisited, or, Very Poor Legs for a Kilt (WG)

Fine Lines: The Process of Creativity – (delivered to the Bristol Medico-Chirurgical Society 8/12/1999)

Stroud Talk (undated? given as judge of children's poetry competition)

Fanthorpe on Fanthorpe

'The Monet Project' in Harry Chambers (ed.) *Poetry Matters 2*, Autumn 1984: 26

'Slow Learner' in Harry Chambers (ed.) *Poetry Matters 5*, Winter 1987: 34-5 (reprinted in Wainwright 1995 Appendix A 66-8)

'Scenes from a Provincial Life' *Country Living* 51, March 1990 (includes 'Wotton Walks') 161-2

'A Hanging Matter' (on *Neck-verse*) *PBS Bulletin* Summer 1992:13 (AHM) (reprinted in Brown and Paterson, 2003: 79-80)

'Poet's Weekend Diary: Lines on the Open Road' *The Guardian* 28 May 1994:16 (re Oxford Election of Professor of Poetry)

'Cold Start' in Raitt S (ed.) *Volcanoes and Pearl Divers: Essays in Lesbian Feminist Studies*, Onlywomen Press 1994:1-12

'Safe As houses?' *Poetry Book Society Bulletin*, Winter 1995 no 167:6

'Walking in Darkness' in *Open Mind* No 83 Jan/Feb 1997: 20-21 (Also collected in *Mind Readings: Writer's Journeys Through Mental States*, Minerva, 1997)

'The evolution of a poem' (on 'Christmas Traffic') The 'A' level English Magazine e issue 2, 1998:14-15

'Hospital Speak: The Neuro-psychiatric Unit' in Alison Mark and Deryn Rees-Jones (eds.) *Contemporary Women's Poetry: Reading/ Writing/ Practice*, Macmillan, Basingstoke, 2000

'War, Poetry, the Child' (WPC) in Herbert and Hollis (eds.) *Strong Words: Modern Poets On Modern Poetry* , Bloodaxe, Newcastle, 2000: 208-210

'Heart of Oak' about *Consequences* in *PBS Bulletin* Summer 2000:14

the e questionnaire in the A-level English magazine Summer 2000:70

'Election 2001: Why I wish I was voting Green', *The Guardian*, May 29 2001: 16

'A Double Brandy' in Jill Gardiner, *From the Closet to the Screen Women at the Gateways Club, 1945-1985* , Pandora, 2001

Readers' Corner 3, *Acumen 50*, September 2004: 42-45

Critical Studies, Articles, Interviews and Profiles on Fanthorpe

Kathryn Bell, *U.A. Fanthorpe: Order and Marginality* (1999) No.49 in the Bookmark series from The English Association, University of Leicester (Available online at www.le.ac.uk/engassoc/publications/bookmarks/49)

Carole Baldock interviews U. A. Fanthorpe 'Portrait' in *For Poets: Forward Magazine For Writers*, Vol 1.iii Aug/Sept 1999

Barbara Baker *The Way We Write: Interviews with Award-Winning Writers* 2007, Continuum, London: pp 74-82

John Banks, 'Who are U?' *Friends Quarterly* 25:3 London 1988: 97-103

Connie Bensley and Judith Kazantis, 'Dropping Out and Standing To: An Interview with U. A. Fanthorpe', PEN 20, Spring 1986: 18-19

Charles Causley, *Arts South West*, May/June 1979

Doris Corti, (Poetry Workshop - discusses 'The Burren') *Writers News*, March 2000:29-30

Sara Davies Interview, *Arts West*, September 1988

Paul Delaney, 'Hearing The Other: Voices in U.A. Fanthorpe's Poetry' *Christianity and Literature* Vol 46 nos. 3-4 Summer 1997: 319-339

Paul Delaney, 'The Hospital Poetry of U.A. Fanthorpe' in *Teaching Literature and Medicine* 2000, viii, 406. A.H. Hawkins & M. C. McEntyre (eds)

Rowena Fowler (thesis) 'Purple shining lilies: imagining The *Aeneid* in Contemporary Poetry (Forthcoming: Oxford Living Classics: Greece and Rome in Contemporary Poetry). Details at: http://users.ox.ac.uk/ ~ spet1820/vergilwebabs.html

Valerie Grove (profile) 'Smile Please, it's a Fanthorpe' , *The Times*, 3/05/03

Diana Hendry: (interview), *Gloucestershire and Avon Life*, August 1985

Marilyn Hacker: 'Unauthorised Voices: U.A. Fanthorpe and Elma Mitchell' *Grand Street*, 1989 Summer vol 8 (4): 147-164

Frieda Hughes discusses Sisyphus *The Times times2*, 15/01/07: 6

Frieda Hughes discusses 'Spring Afternoon' *The Times times2*, 2/04/07:6

Ruth Padel discusses U.A.F.'s 'Rising Damp' in *52 Ways of Looking at a Poem*, London, Chatto and Windus 2002, p125 (from her weekly column in *The Independent On Sunday*)

Christina Patterson (Profile) 'Life of The English Poet', *The Independent*, 31/10/03: 22-23

Angela Pitt, 'Face to Face: A conversation with U.A. Fanthorpe', *English Review* , 1994 4.4: 10-14

Bernard Richards, 'Comparisons: Seamus Heaney, U. A. Fanthorpe and Carol Ann Duffy', *English Review* 6.4 April 1996: 16-20

Ingrid V Rosenberg, 'De-Constructing a Poem Deconstructing a Myth: U. A. Fanthorpe's 'Not My Best Side' (Uccello: S. George and the Dragon, The National Gallery) *Anglistik Englischunterricht* , Heidelberg, Germany 53, (1994: 63-75)

Elizabeth Sandie, 'Acts of Attention: The Poetry Of U A. Fanthorpe' in Leslie Jeffries and Peter Sansom (eds.), *Contemporary Poems: Some Critical Approaches*, Huddersfield , Smith/Doorstop, 2000:146-168

Elizabeth Sandie, 'Conversations at Wotton' July 2002 (unpublished tape)

Debbie Taylor (interview) *Mslexia*, Autumn 1999: 39-40

Lidia Vianu interviews U.A. Fanthorpe (2002)
http://lidiavianu.bleu.ro/ua_fanthorpe.htm

Desperado Essay-Interviews, University of Bucharest 2006

Eddie Wainwright *Taking Stock: A First Study of The Poetry of U. A. Fanthorpe*, Peterloo, Calstock , 1995 (includes 1993 interview 69-75)

Derek Weeks 'Fanthorpe's Rhyme and Reason' *Gloucestershire and Avon Life*, April 1987

Reviews (in date order – abbreviations refer to collection reviewed)

Charles Causley (SE) in *Arts South West* May June 1979

Diana Hendry (SE) ' Watchwords from the Wards', *Gloucestershire and Avon Life* Aug 1979: 65

Peter Scupham (SE) *PN Review* Vol 6/4 1979

Alan Brownjohn (SE) *Encounter*

Georges Szirtes (ST) *Times Literary Supplement* July15 1983

Glen Cavaliero (ST) *The Present Tense* 4 1983

Linda Anderson (SP) *Writing Women* vol 4 no 2

Anna Adams (SP) *Acumen 4* October 1986

Alan Bold (SP) *The Scotsman* July 5 1986

Simon Rae (SP) *Times Literary Supplement*   November 7 1986

Pam Barnard (SP) *Poetry Wales* 23/1, November 1987

Vernon Scannell (WB) *Poetry Review* Vol 77/4 Winter 1987/8

Hugh Buckingham (WB) *Stand* Winter 87/8: 74-75

Peter Forbes (WB) *The Listener* Feb 25 1987

Roy Fuller (WB) *The Spectator* Jan 30 1988

Lawrence Sail (WB) *Stand* Summer 89: 78

Edwina Burness (WB) 'Unauthorised Versions' *PN Review* 15/3 48-9

John Saunders (VO) *Stand* vol 28/2 Spring 1987: 76

John Mole's reviews collected in *Passing Judgements: Poetry in the Eighties*, Bristol Classical Press, 1989 (includes comments on *Standing To* (p11-12) *Voices Off* (p108-9)

George Szirtes (VO) *Critical Quarterly* Vol 27/2

Sheenagh Pugh in *Poetry Review* 82 no 4 Winter 1993: 56

Carol Ann Duffy (NV) 'Light Terrors' *The Guardian* July 2 1992: 26

Neil Powell (NV) *Times Literary Supplement* Nov 20 1992

David Kennedy (NV) *PN Review* Jan/Feb 1993: 62

Lawrence Sail (NV) *Stand* Spring 1993: 79-80

Anne Born (NV) *Envoi* 103 Autumn 1992

Stephen Knight (NV) *London Magazine* Aug/ Sept 1993

Elizabeth Lowry (SAH) 'Nt fr lng. Nt fr lng' *TLS* March 1 1996: 28

Helen Dunmore (SAH) *Observer* May 26 1996: 16

Lavinia Greenlaw (SAH) *The Guardian* July 26 1996: 16

Michael Foot (SAH) 'You can't teach old cars new tricks' *Back Page* H& H series August 30 1996

Kathleen Jamie (C) in *PBS Bulletin* Summer 2000: 14

Hubert Moore (C) in *North* 27 Winter 2000: 40

Guy Wareing, (C) 'Modest Recording Angel' *Poetry Review* 90/3 Autumn 2000: 69-70

Alan Brownjohn (C) *The Sunday Times* 12/2000 (Culture Section p 42)*

Sally Connolly ' Woolly whispers of the past' *The Times Literary Supplement* 13/4/2001: 25

David Wheatley (Q) 'Shining Example' *Guardian Review* 28/06/03

Alan Brownjohn (Q) 'To Boldly Go' *The Sunday Times* 29/06/03

James Mcgrath, (Q) 'An Act of Rescue: Queueing for the Sun' *PN Review* 30:2 November-December 2003 p.66.

Oliver Dennis: (Ch) 'Haunted Self' *PN Review* (29:4) March-April 2003:79.

W. N. Herbert (CP) *Poetry Book Society Bulletin* Spring 2005:13

Fiona Sampson (CP) June 2005 for Tower Poetry

http://www.towerpoetry.org.uk/poetry-matters/june2005/fanthorpe.html

Peter Forbes (CP) 'Under the Sun' *Poetry Review* 95:2 Summer 2005: 95-7

Sean O'Brien (CP) *The Sunday Times Culture* 01/01/06

Anne Stevenson (CP) 'Poetry in the Feminine Mode' *London Magazine* Dec 05/ Jan06: 115-121

John Greening (CP) 'An eye for the times' *Times Literary Supplement* 05/05/06: 26

Secondary Reading

Julian Andrews, *London's War: The Shelter Drawings of Henry Moore*, Aldershot, Lund Humphries, 2002

Isobel Armstrong, *Victorian Poetry: Poetry, Politics, Poetics*, Routledge, 1993. *Nineteenth-Century Women Poets*, Oxford University Press, 1996.

Margaret Atwood, *Negotiating with the Dead: A Writer on Writing*, CUP, 2002

Barbara Baker *The Way We Write: Interviews with Award-winning Writers*, Continuum, London and New York, 2007

Michael Baxandall, *Shadows and Enlightenment*, Yale, 1995

Gillian Beer, 'End of the Line', *The Guardian Saturday Review* 13/01/07: 21.

Vicki Bertram (ed.) *Kicking Daffodils: Twentieth-Century Women Poets*, 1997

Alan Bleasdale, *Boys from the Blackstuff*, Hutchinson, London, 1985

Barbara Blenheim (ed) *Five Modern Poets: Fleur Adcock, U.A. Fanthorpe, Tony Harrison, Anne Stevenson, Derek Walcott*

Jean Binta Breeze 'Ordinary Mawning' in *Riddym Ravings*, Race Today, London, 1988

Melvyn Bragg, *The Adventure of English: The Biography of a Language*, Sceptre, 2003

Clare Brown and Don Paterson (eds.) *Don't Ask Me What I Mean; Poets in Their Own Words*, Picador, 2003

Eavan Boland *Object Lessons: the Life of the Woman and the Poet In Our Time*, Vintage, London, 1996

Peter Childs, *The Twentieth-Century in Poetry*, Routledge, London, 1999

Alan Clark , 'Past Tense, History, Heritage and Ideology' In *Britishness and Cultural Studies: Continuity and Change in Narrating the Nation*, editied by Krystof Knauer and Simon Murray, Katowice, 2000 pp70-81

Kate Clanchy, *Newborn*, Picador, 2004

Julia Copus, 'Beyond the Bell Jar' in *Poetry Review* vol.86, no 4, Winter 1996/7:10

Neil Corcoran, *English Poetry Since 1940*, Longman, Harlow, 1993

Jeni Couzyn, *The Bloodaxe Book of Contemporary Women Poets*, Newcastle, 1985

Gary Day and Brian Docherty (eds.) *British Poetry form the 1950's to the 1990's: Politics and Art*, Macmillan, Basingstoke, 1997

Nicholas de Jongh, *Not In Front Of The Audience, Homosexuality on Stage* Routledge, 1992

Jane Dowson, 'Older Sisters are Very Sobering Things: Contemporary Women Poets and the Female Affiliation Complex', *Feminist Review* No 62 Summer 1999: 6-20; *Women, Modernism and British Poetry, 1910-1939*, Ashgate Aldershot, 2002

Jane Dowson and Alice Entwistle, *A History of Twentieth-Century British Women's Poetry*, Cambridge University Press, 2005

Mary Eagleton, *Feminist Criticism* Balckwell, Oxford (1995); *Working with Feminist Criticism* (1996)

Terry Eagleton, *How to Read a Poem*, Blackwell, Oxford, 2007

T.S. Eliot, *Four Quartets*, Faber, 1959

Gary Geddes (ed) *Twentieth-Century Poetry and Poetics* (4th Edition) 1996

Gelpi BC and Gelpi A (eds) *Adrienne Rich's Poetry and Prose*, Norton, New York , 1993

E.H. Gombrich *Shadows: The Depiction of Cast Shadows in Western Art*, 1995

Lise Gotfredsen, *The Unicorn* , London, The Harvill Press, 1999

Germaine Greer: *Slipshod Sybils: Recognition, Rejection and the Woman Poet*, New York Viking, 1995

Radclyffe Hall, *The Well Of Loneliness* (1928)

Michael Handford and David Viner Stroudwater *Thames and Severn Canals Towpath Guide*, Gloucester 1984

Herbert and Hollis (eds) *Strong Words: Modern Poets On Modern Poetry* Bloodaxe, Newcastle, 2000

Margaret Homans, *Women Writers and Poetic Identity*, Princeton, 1980

Hulse et al, *The New Poetry*, Bloodaxe, Newcastle, 1993

Kathleen Jamie, *Mr and Mrs Scotland Are Dead*, Bloodaxe, Newcastle, 2002

Jackie Kay, 'In Conversation with Richard Dyer', *Wasafiri* 29, 1999: 57.

Graham Kershaw, *Poetraits*, Ledbury, 2003

Julia Kristeva, *Black Sun: Depression and Melancholia*, New York, 1989

David Kennedy, *New Relations: The Refashioning of British Poetry 1980- 94*, Seren, Bridgend, 1996

Philip Larkin, *Collected Poems*, The Marvell Press and Faber , London, 1988

Hermione Lee *Body Parts: Essays on Life–writing*, Chatto and Windus, London, 2005

John Lucas, *Harry Chambers & Peterloo Poets*, 2009

Hilary Mantel 'No Passport Required' *The Guardian Review*, 12/10/02:4-6

Alison Mark and Deryn Rees-Jones (eds) *Contemporary Women's Poetry: Reading/ Writing/ Practice*, Basingstole, Macmillan, 2000

John Mole, *Passing Judgements: Poetry in the Eighties: Essays from Encounter*, Bristol, 1989

Jan Montefiore, *Feminisim and Poetry: Language Experience and Identity in Women's Poetry*, (fully revised and updated with an introduction by Claire Buck), Pandora, London, 2004; 'Women and Tradition', *The Poetry Review*, Vol 94.2 Summer 2004: 58-68

Brian Moynahan, *William Tyndale: If God Spare My Life*, Abacus, 2003

Sean O'Brien, *The Deregulated Muse: Essays on Contemporary British and Irish Poetry*, Bloodaxe, Newcastle, 1998

Ruth Padel, *52 Ways of Looking at a Poem*, Chatto, London, 2002

Tom Paulin, *Writing to the Moment: Selected Critical Essays 1980-1996*, Faber, London, 1996

Ed Picot, *Outcasts from Eden: Ideas of Landscape in British Poetry since 1945*, 1997

Suzanne Raitt (ed) *Volcanoes and Pearl Divers: Essays in Lesbian Feminist Studies*, Onlywomen Press, London, 1995

Deryn Rees-Jones (ed), *Modern Women Poets*, Bloodaxe, Newcastle, 2005; *Consorting With Angels: Essays on Modern Women Poets*, Bloodaxe, Newcastle, 2005

Eliza E Rathbone in Charles S Moffett et al, *Impressionists in Winter: Effets de Neige*, Washington, 1999

Nick Rennison & Michael Schmidt (eds), *Poets on Poets*, Carcanet, Manchester, 1997

Adrienne Rich 'When we Dead Awaken' in *Poetry and Prose Selected and edited by BC Gelpi and A Gelpi*, Norton, New York, 1993

Tim Robinson (ed) Notes and Introduction, *The Burren: A two inch map of the uplands of north-west Clare Folding Landscapes*, Roundstone, Galway, 1999

Carol Rumens, *Making for The Open*, Chatto, 1985, 2nd edition1987. *Self into Song*: Newcastle, Bloodaxe Poetry Lectures, 2007

Elizabeth Sandie, 'Stepping Out into the Twenty First Century: British Women Poets Heading for Planet Alice' in Knauer and Murray (eds) *Britishness and Cultural Studies: Continuity and Change in Narrating the Nation* Katowice, 2000

Laura Severin, *Poetry Off the Page: Twentieth-Century British Women Poets In Performance*, Aldershot, Ashgate, 2004

Joanne Shattock (ed.) *Women and Literature in Britain 1800-1900*, 2001, CUP

Zadie Smith, 'Fail better' in *The Guardian Saturday Review*, 13/01/07.

'Read Better' 20/01/07

Antony Storr, *Churchill's Black Dog and Other Phenomena of the Human Mind*, Glasgow, 1990

Antony Thwaite, *Poetry Today: A Critical Guide to British Poetry 1960-1995* Longman in association with the British Council, 1996

Marina Warner, lecture edited in *Guardian Review* 06/08/05

Liz Yorke, *Impertinent Voices: Subversive Strategies in Contemporary Women's Poetry* Routledge, London, 1991. 'British Lesbian Poetics: A brief exploration' in *Feminist Review* 62, Summer 1999

Other Resources

Dramatisation multi-media

Credo Community Arts, 'Self-Assembly' 1st performed 15/11/1998 Hull Revived *riverlines* York 15/03/03 http://www.credoarts.org.uk/

Television Profile

Leslie Pitt and Patrick Taggart (directors), 'Under the Edge' February 1998 (TV profile - 1/8-part *West Foot Forward* series of celebrity walks for HTV.)

CDs and Cassettes

U.A. Fanthorpe and Elma Mitchell, Peterloo, 1983, *Awkward Subject*, Peterloo, 1995 (now available on CD)
Double Act (with R.V. Bailey) Penguin, 1997
The Bloodaxe Poetry Quartets (5) (with Elizabeth Jennings, Helen Dunmore and Jo Shapcott) (1999)
U.A.Fanthorpe Reading From her Poems, Poetry Archive, (Poetry Book Society) CD http://www.poetryarchive.org

Internet

2005 interview for the National Poetry Archive http://www.poetryarchive.org/
Peter Forbes gives a critical perspective on the British Council's Contemporary Writers website: www.contemporarywriters.com

Musical Settings

Tony Noakes has set several of The Christmas poems; Howard Goodall (better known for his work on the Rowan Atkinson series) set 'All the Queen's Horses' a commission for the 2002 proms; The Bristol Triptych was set by Nigel Dodd;

Images

Jemimah Kuhfeld's portrait of U.A.Fanthorpe formed part of a 2009 exhibition "Photographic Portraits of Poets" at The National Portrait Gallery.
A digital photograph portrait (2004) by Mark Gerson also hangs in The National Portrait Gallery (NPGx 126433).
A portrait by Graham Kershaw appears in his *Poetraits*, (Ledbury, 2003, 34-5) together with Fanthorpe's poem, "Faced".
Sketches of Fanthorpe and Bailey by Judy Collins at the Under The Edge Poetry Reading 12/12 /03 appear at www.undertheedgearts.org.uk/

Archive material

The University of Gloucestershire
www.glos.ac.uk/departments/lit/archives archives@glos.ac.uk

INDEX

Index of titles of individual poems cited

Writers / Writing

Elizabeth Sandie

Photograph by Jen Todman